Da Nang and Hoi An, Vietnam

My Saigon, Volume 6

Elly Thuy Nguyen

Published by Elly Thuy Nguyen, 2025.

DA NANG AND HOI AN, VIETNAM

First edition. January 22, 2025.

Copyright © 2025 Elly Thuy Nguyen.

ISBN: 978-1543287608

Written by Elly Thuy Nguyen.

Also by Elly Thuy Nguyen

My Saigon
My Saigon: The Local Guide to Ho Chi Minh City, Vietnam
Secrets to Live in Vietnam on $500 a Month
Da Nang and Hoi An, Vietnam
Dating Vietnamese Women
Happy in Hanoi: The Local Guide to Hanoi, Vietnam
Undiscovered Quy Nhon: The Local Guide to Vietnam's Beach Paradise
Discover Dalat: Local Travel Guide to Da Lat, Vietnam

Table of Contents

Introduction to the 2025 edition 1

Five Danang pluses 5

Five Danang minuses 7

Very basic Vietnamese language 9

Obligatory "Getting There" and visas 13

Money, shopping, and tipping 19

Getting mobile data 27

Getting around Danang 31

Geographic overview, and where to stay in Danang 37

Hotel recommendations 41

Cafes aren't just for coffee 51

Waterfront sugar fix 65

Get your beer on 71

The hair wash of a lifetime (plus massage) 75

Live music 77

Bridges! Breathing! Fire! And Spinning! 81

Eating Street 85

Other eats 91

Uniquely Vietnamese: Cao Dai temple 101

Musea 103

Beaches and surfing 105

Serious seafood 111

Marble Mountains 115

Danang now has tourist traps! 121

Ba Na: cable cars to pseudo-Europe 125

Getting from Danang to Hoi An 139

Hoi An overview 147

Walking through Hoi An Old Town 151

Hoi An Tailors 159

Love it 161

Introduction to the 2025 edition

This is the 2025 edition. It's basically all new. The word count has doubled since the 2023 edition, and that's after I deleted most of the 2023-vintage text, simply because it's no longer relevant. Danang has changed and this book has kept pace.

I've also added a lot more photos now. Because I have a much better camera in 2025 than I did in 2023 and definitely than in 2017. Seriously, that's the reason.

Danang has grown and developed tremendously since this guide's original release in 2017, and even since the 2023 update. I was on to something when in 2017 I thought the world could use a local guide to Danang.

This 2025 edition is greatly expanded. I've added a lot of places that didn't exist back in 2023, and some other places that I just hadn't managed to include in 2023. Other places have dropped off my recommendation list — not just those that closed down, but those that declined in quality, or just simply no longer make the cut in the bigger, better, more competitive Danang of 2025.

In this 2025 update, in addition to more information about central Danang, I've added a lot more detail on Hoi An, Ba Na Hills, and Marble Mountains. I've also covered more of the city of Danang, as it's expanded more beyond its core. I've scouted out a few interesting hotels for you. And I've found even more great places to eat, because of course.

With this fresh, delicious info, you'll make the best of Danang, Hoi An, and wherever your central-Vietnam explorations take you.

Danang has beaches, unspoiled Vietnamese culture, mountains, food, and nearby are the magical small streets and lantern-illuminated canals of Hoi An. You want to go, right?

Twenty years ago, Vietnamese people would've told you you're crazy. Now, tourism in Danang is booming. It's booming mostly for Vietnamese and Korean tourists, but still, it's booming. People love this place that's not as hot as Saigon, not as crowded as Hanoi, and much cheaper and more orderly than both of them.

Danang used to be the ugly stepsister to Hanoi and Saigon, unknown and unloved not only by foreign tourists but even by us Vietnamese people. It used to be a small town, even a dumpy town, far down on anybody's list. In US terms, it was pretty much Vietnam's Cleveland. Now, it's Vietnam's... Portland? Something like that.

Danang is Vietnam's third city, and it's hot. Partly it's hot because it's not too hot: as global warming and Vietnamese pollution ramp up, Danang retains its mostly cool, clean air. Everybody (in Vietnam, at least) wants to visit Danang. But Danang retains some of its small-town inscrutability (and perhaps charm), in that information about it is hard to find, even in Vietnamese.

Even for us Vietnamese people, the only real way to find out about Danang is "my friend's aunt used to live there, and she says" or "my brother went there a few years ago, and he took pictures of a cool coffee shop, but he doesn't remember the name."

Even Google Maps / Google Reviews for Danang is full of mistakes, wrong addresses, wrong hours, unlisted places, and listings of long-closed-down places.

And the other English-language sources? They pretty much go "Dana-HOI AN HOI AN HOI AN!" Poor Danang. Danang isn't well documented. At all. Even Hoi An suffers, because the people writing about it are tourists who don't speak Vietnamese and don't know much about the larger context of Vietnam. This book changes everything.

This book is a local's guide to Danang, insofar as it reflects what I've found through my multiple visits and stays there, and what I've been told by my Danang-dwelling friends and contacts. As with my guide to Saigon, this guide will focus on what a local would consider best in their city.

This guide is skewed to Vietnamese tastes. But isn't that the only way to write a local guide to a Vietnamese city? Don't worry: no Vietnamese linguistic or cultural knowledge is required.

This guide also covers Hoi An. But I don't let Hoi An completely steal the spotlight from Danang. Hoi An is a lot of fun, but just as you shouldn't forget about Dre, you also shouldn't forget about Danang.

I strongly recommend not ignoring Danang, even if your initial interest is Hoi An, because Danang is a real Vietnamese city, pretty much unspoiled or unchanged by mass tourism (aside from a few beaches full of Chinese and Korean tour buses). Spend a few days in Danang, following my local suggestions, and you will have had as much a real Vietnamese experience as anyone could have had—certainly more real than the backpacker-centric, tourist-oriented experience you'd have if you stayed exclusively in Hoi An.

We Vietnamese people don't avoid Hoi An, but we see it as an amusement park. It's nice to visit for a few hours, but you wouldn't want to live in an amusement park, and you probably wouldn't want to spend your entire vacation inside the amusement park either. Yet, unfortunately, most Westerners treat Danang as only a gateway to the Hoi An amusement park.

This is a local's guide, so I encourage you to treat Hoi An as a nice amusement park, but not to limit yourself to Hoi An. Explore Danang. It's a real Vietnamese city. It's definitely the least touristy of Vietnam's cities. There's also something purely Vietnamese about Danang: it lacks the strong Cantonese and American influence of Saigon and the strong Mainland Chinese and Russian influence of Hanoi, as well as the hordes of Russian tourists you'd find in Nha Trang and Mui Ne and the hordes of Chinese tourists you'd find in Phu Quoc. Da Nang is about as authentic as it gets.

The local suggestions in this guide will be useful even for a Vietnamese person who wants to experience Danang. Contrary to popular belief, we Vietnamese people don't automatically know everything about everywhere in Vietnam. We need guidebooks too, and usually the Vietnamese-language ones are thinly veiled advertising. So this is a book that would be useful not only for foreign visitors, but even for my Vietnamese friends who want to know Danang.

This is your boutique insider's guide to the local lowdown on Danang and Hoi An, like having a very talkative Vietnamese friend: me. It's an in-depth local take that no other guide provides.

Five Danang pluses

1. It's cleaner, quieter, and safer than Saigon and Hanoi. Trash cans are in actual use here; in Saigon and Hanoi, people throw their garbage on the street. Car and motorcycle horns are not in constant use in Danang. You don't hear motorcycle engines day and night. You can actually walk on some of the sidewalks, sometimes; they're not always taken up by motorcycle parking (or even worse, motorcycle traffic) as they are in Saigon and Hanoi. And if you walk around with your purse, camera, or phone dangling at your side (not recommended anywhere in the world, but especially not recommended in Hanoi and Saigon), you are quite likely to return home with your property still yours! Imagine that.

2. Beach to city? Ten minutes. City to mountains? Thirty minutes. You can't even do this in Seattle or LA! The Danang area has beaches and mountains immediately adjoining the central urban area. The geography is quite compressed, and traffic is never too terrible—at least not by Vietnamese standards. So you can have a change of environment very quickly.

3. Bowl of noodles in the middle of the city? 30,000 VND. Haircut? 30,000 VND. Cup of coffee? 30,000 VND. That's 1 USD. Prices for many things are about half the level in Saigon or Hanoi.

4. People smoke less than in Hanoi and especially Saigon. For me, it's a huge thing. In Saigon it's unthinkable to have any evening gathering spot without a thick cloud of smoke. In Danang, even if smoking isn't expressly prohibited, not many people smoke. Don't get your hopes up: almost all men in Danang do smoke. They're just not the Saigonese smoke-belchers I'm used to.

5. According to the Danang city government, in Danang, there are no homeless people, no drug addicts, no beggars, and no poor people. Now that you've recovered from your laughter: while those claims are exaggerated, you will find many fewer beggars and street people in Danang than in Hanoi or Saigon. Maybe it's just because there are fewer tourists in Danang as opposed to those cities, or maybe because

the gaps between rich and poor aren't so wide (my theory is it's because all Danang's very rich and very poor have left Danang for Saigon or Hanoi). But you can spend an entire vacation as a tourist in Danang and not be approached by beggars even once.

Five Danang minuses

No place is perfect. I like visiting Danang, but I can't imagine living there. My complaints about Danang mostly come down to it being still like a small town or village. I like cities. Danang is Vietnam's third-biggest city, but it sometimes feels like a remote village.

1. Everything runs on erratic Danang time, even more so than in the rest of Vietnam. Businesses open and close pretty much when they feel like it. Don't be surprised if a well-regarded local business is closed for a week because the owner's cousin is visiting from Saigon or because a waitress is sick. Don't be surprised if a business that claims to be open 24/7 is open only a few hours a day. And so on. If a business in Danang has opening hours posted on its door or online, consider those hours to be a best-case goal that's seldom actually accomplished.

2. For a Saigonese person, Danang is freezing cold most of the year. Sure, there's a "beach," but for half the year, around September until March, the beach has clouds and rainstorms and is much too cold to swim, even for local Danang people. Expect temperatures in the 50s Fahrenheit (10 - 15 Celsius) much of the year. It's not Arctic cold, but it's not beach weather either. I wonder about the Korean tourists who visit Danang on "beach vacations" during the winter. Don't expect much sunshine any time of year. You see the Seattle comparison here?

3. Service is not great. Most people are really used to their traditional village lives and never shopped in stores or went to cafes or restaurants until quite recently. And there's not really a customer service culture. It's more like "Well I gave you your food, didn't I?" and that's the end of it. Even more so if you appear to be foreign, as most service staff are terrified of their lack of English ability, and instead of trying to make do with basic English or Vietnamese or Google Translate, they just avoid foreign customers. Don't be surprised if some waitstaff literally pretend not to see you. They're just terrified of "having to speak English." In Vietnam, even today, the penalty for giving a wrong answer in school (e.g. when told to speak English) can be a physical

beating. For most non-elite students in Vietnam, school is all about trying to hide from the teacher and avoid being asked questions (and therefore avoid beatings for wrong answers) — that persists in the workplace, more so in Danang (and in rural areas) than in the bigger cities.

4. Danang people are... not Saigonese. The culture is much chillier in Danang than in Saigon. Danang people remind me of Hanoi people. In fact, according to some Saigonese know-it-alls, Danang people are even chillier than Hanoi people. If I make a dumb joke to a cafe waiter in Saigon, he'll joke back and we'll spend a few minutes kidding around and being silly. If I make a dumb joke to a cafe waiter in Danang, I'll get a polite smile and nothing more. If I buy a banh mi from the same street seller in Saigon three days in a row, she'll ask me what I do for a living, why I'm not married, and whether I want to go drink coffee with her and her family that evening. If I buy a banh mi from the same street seller in Danang three days in a row, she'll give me my sandwich and send me on my way. And so on. It's not better or worse, but it's a different culture from Saigon.

5. 10 P.M.? Beddy bye bye! In Saigon, most things are closed after 10 P.M., but there is still a vibrant street culture at all hours, especially for eating, drinking coffee, sitting with friends while drinking fruit juice, or just sitting somewhere and chatting. In Danang, everything (except nightclubs) is really, seriously, totally closed around 10.

Very basic Vietnamese language

Yes, you can travel in Vietnam without speaking a word of Vietnamese. You can also visit Antarctica without gloves. In both cases, you'll survive, but you'll have a not-so-great experience.

Tourists to Vietnam aren't supposed to know *any* Vietnamese. So if you can manage twenty basic words or phrases, you will be way, way ahead of everyone else. You will also have a wider range of options in everything (since you won't depend on only English-speaking places), you will have fewer misunderstandings, you will likely have more respect from people, and you will be more likely to be on your way to warmer, better treatment by Vietnamese people. Trust me on this one.

I don't think there is much point to learning the standard things in Vietnamese phrasebooks, which will teach you useful phrases such as "What a lovely vegetable garden you have," and "I wish to be medically evacuated." (Back in the old hardline communist days in Vietnam, phrasebooks taught crucial terms such as "black-marketeer," "commune," and "American puppet regime." You might still be able to find a phrasebook like that on some dusty back shelf in a Vietnamese bookstore, if you're really, really bored.)

Here's what you need to know: really basic terms, and, most importantly, numbers. Numbers are for prices of course.

Basic terms:

Chao - hi

Cam on - thank you

Bao nhieu (tien)? - how much (money)?

X o dau? - where is X?

Nuoc suoi - water

Ve sinh - bathroom

Phong - room (like a hotel room)

Khach san - hotel

San bay - airport

Tap hoa - convenience store

Xe - car or motorcycle or any vehicle

Khong can - I don't want it

(Muon) mua - (want to) buy
Numbers:
Le (or, in formal speech, Khong) - zero
Mot - one
Hai - two
Ba - three
Bon (or, when referring to people, Tu) - four
Nam - five
Sau - six
Bay - seven
Tam - eight
Chin - nine
Muoi - ten
Tram - hundred
Ngan - thousand
Trieu - million

You make bigger numbers by combining what you already know. For example, 1,111,111 would be "mot trieu, mot tram muoi mot ngan, mot tram muoi mot"—translated word-for-word to English as "one million, one hundred eleven thousand, one hundred eleven."

Also, in common Vietnamese slang when dealing with money, the slang term "chuc" is used to mean "ten" or "ten thousand." So the formally correct way to say 50,000 VND would be "nam muoi ngan," but in slang, people say "nam chuc" or "nam chuc ngan." And US dollars are called "do." So a slangy way to say "fifty dollars" would be "nam chuc do."

That's it. Now you know the numbers and basic words and are way ahead of almost all other visitors to Vietnam.

There are a few other things you should know: what's written on signs.

Bac si - physician

Bang gia - price list (this is an important bit of knowledge; often a business will have a price list posted, and you can check the price list to see whether you're being overcharged—this even holds true in places like train stations where they sell tickets)

Cam - prohibited / keep out

Canh sat / Cong an - police

Duong - street

Hem - alley

Khong hut thuoc - no smoking (hooray!)

Mien phi - free

Ngan hang - bank

Nha hang - restaurant

Phong kham - medical clinic (this is important should you get into an accident; small clinics are very cheap and, for basic cuts and bruises, very competent—but they rarely have any English signage, so you might have no idea it's a medical clinic)

Obligatory "Getting There" and visas

The following is an exhaustive list of direct and connecting flights into Danang, and the telephone and fax numbers of several reputable airlines. Just kidding. Guidebooks still include long, boring passages about what airlines fly there from what cities, how much airfares cost, and phone numbers to airlines. Thanks; I'll bring travelers' checks so I can tip the stewardess for my martini. On the Concorde. In the smoking section. I'll fax you the Polaroids.

I won't give you all that boomertastic info. I assume you have an internet connection. And if you don't, you've got bigger problems than what to do in Danang. But I'll tell you this: Danang airport is growing just as much as the city is. There are now nonstop flights from all over Asia, especially Korea, and Danang is a true international airport—you can get your electronic visa or visa-on-arrival in Danang, and the immigration lines and waits are generally much faster than in Saigon or Hanoi. Hooray.

Danang was the world's busiest airport during the Vietnam War. Danang was a major base of US military operations. After the war, it became a sleepy domestic airport again—until the past few years, when it's become a booming hub again, this time mostly hosting tourist arrivals from Asia, especially China as the biggest tourist market, and Korea as a distant second. There are actually nonstop flights to Danang even from small cities in China and Korea—that's how popular it has become for Asian tourists.

If you're flying in to Vietnam, Danang is a good choice of entry point, because it's geographically central and immigration processing is easier and faster than Saigon, except that flights to Danang do tend to be more expensive than to Saigon, simply because there's less competition. It's often actually cheaper to get an international flight into Saigon, then separately fly into Danang.

What airline to take from Saigon (or Hanoi) to Danang? Putatively, your three choices are Vietjet, Bamboo, and Vietnam Airlines. Please take Vietnam Airlines. Please. And no, I don't have any relatives working there (Vietnam Airlines only hires Northerners anyway).

Vietnamese low-cost carriers are notorious for terrible service, itineraries completely changed at the last minute (congratulations, you missed your flight, because you didn't know we rescheduled you to fly yesterday, not today!), and long delays. Vietnam Airlines is pretty good about staying on time, and they've certainly gotten better since the bargain competitors came around.

Some of that difference is of the bargain airlines' own doing and the way they operate, with the only contingency plan for equipment failures or staff absences being "delay some flights." But part of it is that the Vietnamese government owns Vietnam Airlines and also owns the airports and the air traffic control systems in Vietnam, and The Important People (the ones who make sure we are all equal) fly Vietnam Airlines, so yeah. Just take Vietnam Airlines.

A roundtrip ticket between Saigon and Danang will cost you about $100 on Vietnam Airlines, while on Not Yet Jet and Bamboozle it would cost you about $60. None of these airlines plays nice with the global online reservation systems, so visit their websites directly (https://www.vietnamairlines.com/) rather than Expedia. Vietnam Airlines does offer its tickets on the international sites, but they are about twice the price of its local website. Also, I recommend you buy any airline tickets in Vietnam with your US credit card, because there are no consumer protections in Vietnam, and if a flight is canceled, you don't automatically get your money back. At least if you use your US credit card, you can dispute the charge. (You see why we Vietnamese people always want to move to the US?)

There are also trains and buses from Saigon and Hanoi to Danang. Don't. Unless you're a masochistic YouTuber or something, just don't. The price of bus and train tickets is about the same as a plane, and the tickets are hard to buy. The official-looking English-language websites claiming to sell Vietnamese train and bus tickets are just dudes who take your money and promise to buy your ticket for you. The arrival times are unpredictable, the toilets are nonexistent or overflowing, the cabins are smelly, and you'll spend an entire day on a Vietnamese train or bus. Any photos or brochures they show you are lies. Sometimes they even have a nice bus pick you up at their terminal, then drive you down the road to the *real* bus that will transport you. Just don't, please. Airplanes were invented for a reason. And as I told you, Vietnam doesn't have consumer protections, so don't expect compensation from the company.

Good news for airplane fans! The Danang airport is pretty much in the middle of the city. Depending on where you're going from the airport, you will pay only around 50,000 VND for a Grab car between the airport and your destination in the city (Hai Chau area) or around 100,000 VND between the airport and the beach areas. Grab Car is by far the best option. Vietnamese taxis are all scammers nowadays. You should download the Grab app before coming to Vietnam.

At the Danang airport domestic terminal, to get a ride to your hotel, meet your Grab driver by the big sign out in the parking lot that (as of this writing) says *Viettel 5G New Life*. The Grab app also tells you to go there, but the way it gives you directions is super complicated. You just need to step outside the terminal and go out until you see that sign up there, and your Grab driver will meet you there.

Tips for the Grab app: You can verify your account either with a Vietnamese phone number, or by WhatsApp with your non-Vietnamese phone number. Grab does take credit cards but — ***and this is not explained anywhere on their site, in their app, nor by their customer service*** — to add a credit card to your Grab app, you must be physically in Vietnam according to your phone's GPS. If you're not physically in Vietnam when you try to add a credit card, you'll get a mysterious error message.

In Danang, change your money to VND at the airport. In Saigon, I would recommend waiting until you get into the city, but there aren't many money changers in Danang outside the airport, so you should stick to the airport. When you leave the international terminal and go outside, make a sharp left turn and go up the small ramp. There are some money changers. The one I recommend is the very first one you see, with a logo that says MB. That's Military Bank. Yes, the Vietnamese military owns a bank. I don't understand it either. Anyway, MB Bank is actually pretty good to deal with, and this money exchange has good rates, friendly service, and only a tiny markup for USD.

If your home currency is something other than USD, you may want to consider bringing USD (or Euros or KRW) instead. The bank will definitely change most any currency you bring (ok, sorry, my Zimbabwean friends), but the rates won't be so great for "rare" currencies, and the amounts they'll change may be limited.

And Vietnam, especially outside Saigon, runs on cash. Don't expect to use credit cards other than in your hotel. Even in your hotel, unless you're staying at a Hyatt or other US chain, they will most likely only accept Visa cards, and not Amex or Discover or other brands.

There are lots of ATMs for dispensing cash in Danang. They will work fine with your home country's ATM card as long as it's a Visa card, and as long as your bank doesn't flag your account for fraud because there's someone using it in Vietnam! Withdrawal limits tend to be around 5 million VND (about $200) and machines tend to tack on a surcharge of about 100K VND. The ATM I recommend, HSBC at 1 Nguyen Van Linh, does dispense up to 15 million VND, with a surcharge of 200K VND.

And don't expect to use USD cash in Vietnam, despite what the guidebooks say; USD fell out of common use in Vietnam about twenty years ago, as VND was no longer subject to wild inflation and rampant counterfeiting. If a shop prices in USD, it's a sure sign of a tourist trap.

You probably need a visa to go to Vietnam, although citizens of some European and Asian countries can enter visa-free (see Wikipedia: https://en.wikipedia.org/wiki/Visa_policy_of_Vietnam).

The easiest way to get a visa is to buy a print-it-yourself "e-visa" online from the Vietnamese government. Pay $25 with your credit card online, submit a digital photo of yourself and of your passport info, and about a week later you'll receive a PDF of an actual visa (not just an approval letter) in your email about a week later. Remember to carry the printed PDF with you. Your airline will demand to see it before they let you board. At the actual Vietnam immigration checkpoint, they do require the printed PDF of your visa, but if you don't have it, they can, uh, "print it for you" for twenty USD or so.

The official Vietnamese government website URL for applying for the visa is https://evisa.gov.vn/

Please note that there are many fakes of this Vietnamese government website, especially using govt.vn addresses. The Vietnamese government uses gov.vn, not govt.vn. Anything at a govt.vn address is merely cosplaying as the Vietnamese government. (Of all the things you could pretend to be, why — ok, never mind.)

When you arrive at the Danang airport with this visa, you don't need to pay anyone or apply for anything—you'll be holding an actual visa that you printed out and can use to enter Vietnam. As in all other countries, you'll need to clear immigration at your first point of entry into the country. So if you're changing planes in Saigon on your way from a foreign country to Danang, you'll need to clear immigration in Saigon.

Saigon immigration can easily take an hour. Danang immigration is usually much, much faster.

They say to allow five working days for the visa to be issued. Based on what I've heard, I would say allow two weeks. Don't apply only a week before your flight, because your boarding the plane will depend on the Vietnamese government following through on its promised processing time. That's a big no no. (And oh wow, Americans complain about the US government?! Anyway.)

Remember the required passport photo is of your passport info page, that has your name and passport number and photo, not of the cover of your passport! Yes, I've heard of people sending a photo of the cover of their passport. (What else, a photo of $25?)

In your face photo, you shouldn't be wearing glasses or a hat, and according to the Vietnamese government, you have to be "straight-looking." (Tee hee! I swear. Check the website. That's what they say.) They just mean you have to be looking right into the camera. Don't worry, our LGBTQA friends are welcome to visit Vietnam.

The photo file requirements are ridiculous: the maximum photo size is 100 kb. Are the visas issued by ants?! Sorry, plz no re-education camp plz plz.

If you don't hear back by email after about a week, you can try emailing them using the form or email address on the website. Sometimes they reply. Usually they don't reply.

Note that sometimes the $25 credit card payment website will give you an error message saying your payment didn't go through, but the charge will go through on your credit card. According to my sources, if this happens, don't worry, and your visa will be fine; there's just a glitch on their website.

You can also use a private visa agent, Vietnam Visa Pro. I suspect all they do is data-enter your info into that same Vietnamese government website. But anyway, they're reliable and trustworthy. They cost about $40 instead of the $25 you'll pay directly to the government. https://vietnamvisapro.net[1]/ (Other websites/companies claiming to be Vietnam Visa Pro are scams.)

If you are ethnically Vietnamese (even only one parent) or married to a Vietnamese citizen, there is supposedly a free five-year "visa exemption certificate" available from the Vietnamese government. The website for applying is http://mienthithucvk.mofa.gov.vn/ . The application process takes six months or so. Go for it if you have lots of time and patience. My Vietnamese American relatives say it's too much trouble to fulfill all the requirements for that and they prefer to just pay $25 or so for a regular visa rather than spend hours on paperwork and weeks corresponding with the Vietnamese government and possibly having to pay bribes that cost more than a regular visa would have cost.

---

1.   https://vietnamvisapro.net/

Money, shopping, and tipping

Currency

Use Vietnamese Dong in Danang. Any sources that tell you to use USD are either twenty years out-of-date or sending you to tourist traps. If you see prices posted in USD or KRW, that's very likely a tourist trap.

Exchange

As mentioned in the previous section on arrivals, you can change your money (preferably USD, Euros, or KRW) into VND at the Da Nang airport, at the MB currency exchange stand, the first one on your left. Don't exchange with any touts yelling "no commission, best rate" — they're quite likely to cheat you, generally relying on you being unable to quickly count how many zeroes are on the currency (giving you a 50,000 note as a 500,000 and so on).

If you want to exchange more money once you're in the city, there aren't really currency exchanges in Da Nang other than at the airport. However, any gold shop — look for a sign saying HIEU VANG, or search for that on Google Maps — will gladly change USD to VND. A gold shop may not be eager to change other currencies for you. Of course, the airport is so close to the city that it would also be reasonable for you to just go to the airport to change more money.

As for the guidebooks that tell you that private currency exchange shops are illegal in Vietnam: they are totally correct! Sort of. That law is completely ignored and there are private currency exchanges openly operating all over the place in Vietnam, especially as part of gold shops. (They probably have to pay a "tax.")

As of 2025, expect about 25,000 VND for 1 USD. Note that you should expect to get a slightly *better* rate for exchanging your USD in Vietnam than what is quoted on Google or other sources. Why? The Google rate is the Bank of Vietnam official rate. But the Bank of Vietnam sells USD only to the Vietnamese government, and it sells USD very cheaply to make our dong look bigger. (I love that joke.) BOV has an artificially bad USD rate, and that's the rate quoted by Google. The street rate in Vietnam is actually better. Not by much, but better. Typically, you'll see Google quote something like 25,100 and the gold shop give you something like 25,500.

Please get rid of all your VND before leaving Vietnam, because it's pretty close to worthless outside of Vietnam. I've seen exchanges in Hong Kong that will give you less than half of the value; in most other places, they won't take it period. If you have spare VND, exchange it back at the airport or give it to your Grab driver or a random airport janitor (who likely makes around $200 a month for 12 hours a day) — or just save it for your next visit to Vietnam.

Note that our liberators forcibly depreciate our currency about 5-10% per year (so that average workers can get yearly "pay raises" that are actually pay cuts), so your VND is guaranteed to be worth less when you come back.

ATMs

ATMs are a good way to get VND. They are all over Danang. My tip is to always use an ATM that is inside of, or attached to, a bank, and preferably during banking hours. It's not uncommon for a Vietnamese ATM to eat your ATM card. If that happens at a standalone ATM on some street corner, you're in trouble. If that happens at an ATM inside a bank, the bank is pretty accustomed to it and will go open the ATM and give you your card back.

Storytime: An ATM in Saigon ate my card. When I told the bank branch staff that the ATM took my debit card, they opened the ATM, and handed me *all three* of the debit cards stuck inside. Two of which weren't mine. And that was when I bought a first-class ticket to North Korea and started my career as an international criminal on the run.

Most ATMs in Vietnam have a withdrawal limit of 2-5 million VND, about $80-200 USD. They add on a surcharge of about 100K VND, $4 USD. Usually the rate your bank uses for the conversion won't be so great. And if the ATM asks you whether you'd like to be charged in your local currency (USD) rather than in VND, always decline that option. It's a way for the bank here in Vietnam to make extra money by giving you a terrible exchange rate instead of letting your bank do the conversion from VND to your home currency.

Recommended ATM: There is an HSBC bank and HSBC ATM at 1 Nguyen Van Linh, in Hai Chau, near the Dragon Bridge. HSBC is the only reputable bank now operating in Vietnam. We had Citibank and ANZ, but they left years ago. HSBC is honest, and its machines at this branch have a 15 million VND ($600 USD) withdrawal limit (subject to your home bank's limit of course), with a 200K VND fee.

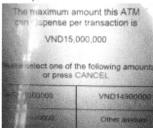

Whenever I've checked, the withdrawal limits have been the same 15 million for both of the machines at this HSBC branch: the machine that says "Express Bank" and the machine that says "ATM." But if you find one machine giving you a low limit, try the other one — they are sometimes set up to have different limits. Welcome to Vietnam!

By the way, the Shinhan Bank down the street advertises a 10 million VND ATM withdrawal limit, but that's only for Vietnamese cards. The limit is only 3 million for foreign cards. Yes, to make you withdraw multiple times and pay multiple fees.

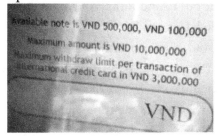

The same is true of most ATMs in Vietnam: if there is a withdrawal limit posted, the limit is usually lower for foreign cards. That HSBC 15 million VND limit is for all cards.

Shopping

You'll hate me for this, but I'm going to tell you to stay away from the "quaint, charming local markets" such as Cho Han and Cho Con in Danang. If anything, you can go there to take some Instagram photos of you roughing it with fish guts splattering all over the place and pickpockets groping your phone. Don't buy anything there. Not even souvenirs. And watch your pockets. And make sure your vaccinations are current. Those places are horrible.

To actually buy anything, go to one of the two big superstores in Danang: LotteMart at 6 Nai Nam

https://maps.app.goo.gl/roeJp9cKtP9PbcR38

or Go! (previously called Big C, and still informally called Big C) at 257 Hung Vuong

https://maps.app.goo.gl/PSNFDNuJEgKS6tXm7

Go! no longer provides a free shuttle bus to and from Hoi An, as they used to provide before covid. (Use either a Grab Car or a Bus Route 02 to get to Hoi An. More info in the Hoi An section. Avoid using one of the heavily-advertised-in-English tourist shuttle bus services for the trip: they are almost the same price as a Grab Car, with all the comfort and convenience of a city bus.)

At Lotte or Go! superstores you'll have a better environment, lower prices, and better stuff than any of the "traditional markets" or street vendors. They do sell lots of souvenirs, including all kinds of snacks that make great small gifts for bringing back from Vietnam.

It's kind of amusing to me: back home in your country, do you prefer to go to a regular, clean, air-conditioned supermarket, or to a dodgy smelly wet market? So why do you think we Vietnamese people are any different? (Yeah, "noble savages" and all that.)

For the equivalent of a convenience store in Danang, look (or search Google Maps) for a sign saying Tap Hoa. Tap Hoa don't really look like convenience stores. It's not like Saigon that's full of chain convenience stores like Circle K. Danang still has the traditional Vietnamese convenience stores called tap hoa. They generally don't have air-conditioning, are kind of haphazard in layout, and their primary sales are usually from alcohol and cigarettes (but isn't that all convenience stores?). Still, they sell snacks, water, toiletries, and other stuff you may need. Prices are, of course, usually totally unmarked and highly variable, so make sure you know what you're paying and don't assume it's a fair price.

Don't believe the billboards around Danang telling you to shop at VV Mall. Yes, VV Mall is "now open." But it doesn't have any stores. There are literally no stores in this failed, completely empty mall, but it's still being advertised to tourists. They are apparently setting up a tourist trap souvenir store just for all the tourists who cluelessly end up going there.

Laundry

Hotels in Danang have found out that in Korea (where most of Danang's tourists are from), laundry is expensive, and they've started charging absolutely outrageous prices for hotel laundry. Think 200K VND per item. While I am usually willing to pay a little bit over the normal rate for in-hotel laundry (say, 40K VND per kilogram instead of the usual Danang street price of 20K VND per kilogram), I'm not going to pay ten times the normal rate.

So here's the laundry I use when I'm in Danang: La Son at 99 Yen Bai in Hai Chau.

https://maps.app.goo.gl/zW9VaLTLJnZV8wkQ8

This is a drop-off laundry, not a laundromat. It looks like a tiny hole in the wall, and it kind of is. Just go in there and yell and they'll come out and help you. They can speak basic English. They'll have your clothes ready the same evening or the next day, and they can deliver to your hotel. Give them your hotel's business card, because many hotels have nearly identical (or sometimes literally identical) names, and write your room number on it. They charge around 20-50K extra for delivery, depending on how far away your hotel is.

You'll pay something like 20K VND per kilogram for your laundry to be washed and dried. Plus 20-50K VND for delivery. It will be good. They can also clean your athletic shoes and backpacks, for something like 100K a piece. And you won't let the hotel jerk you around like that.

Yes, there are other laundries in Danang, and I'm sure they're fine. I'm just recommending the one I use. Search Google Maps for *giat ui*, which is "laundry and pressing" in Vietnamese, and you'll find them.

Tipping

Is there tipping in Vietnam? Contrary to what most guidebooks say, yes, there is tipping in Vietnam. A lot of it.

I saw a well-regarded guidebook that warned tourists to Vietnam that Vietnamese people will be "insulted" by a tip. I'm not sure if that travel book writer has ever actually met a Vietnamese waiter. Or policeman. Cough cough.

Anyway, enough ragging on the other guidebooks. The point is, in most situations in Vietnam, tips are not expected, but very much appreciated and not all that infrequent.

Everyone, from a street vendor to a shop clerk to a hairstylist to a maid, will very much appreciate a tip. Although VND is always preferred, they'll be happy with your USD. (No US coins, though. Apparently that was the customary way of tipping during the War. But nowadays, coins aren't worth much, and also, they're not accepted by currency exchanges. So if you tip in USD, keep it to paper money.)

How much to tip? The most important tipping tip (see what I did?) is that you should focus on the amount, not on the percentage of the bill. Tipping as a percentage of the bill is in fact a truly foreign concept in Vietnam.

I would say a general default tip is 10K-20K vnd. That's true for restaurants, cafes, taxi drivers, maids, hotel staff, delivery, and even shop clerks and cashiers who have been very helpful. Of course everyone will love it if you tip more, but it's not necessary. Bigshots do give 500K to their baristas, but that's showoff world and you don't need to emulate them. On the other hand, tipping less than 5K ($0.20) might be insulting.

Of course, if someone has spent a lot of time helping you, or you've just had a huge very fancy meal, give them 100K or even 200K if you want. But it's not expected.

The only exception to the rule of 10K-20K is massages. For massages, you should really tip a minimum of 100K, because massage staff in Vietnam generally make *negative* salary. They have to pay to work in a massage shop, and then they have to give the boss a cut of their tips. Welcome to Workers' Paradise! So tip a minimum of 100K, and 200K or even 500K isn't too much.

As much as you can, try to put the tip directly into the worker's hand. Vietnamese bosses will confiscate any tips they can get their hands on. If you leave a tip on the table or especially put it in an official tip jar, consider it gone into the boss's pocket.

Lastly, if you are interested in helping disadvantaged people in Vietnam, do it by tipping people, and *not* by donating to any "charities" or "collection boxes" you see, *even and especially* if they have "official endorsements." All that money tourists donate to good causes goes to the big guys' Bentleys. Trust me. And most of the people working in the service industry in Vietnam come from extremely poor rural backgrounds and would be greatly helped by any small amount of money you can send their way.

Getting mobile data

While free wifi is indeed plentiful in Danang, it's not so plentiful that you can get by without mobile data. You'll still need data when you're not in the confines of your hotel or a cafe or restaurant. That and free wifi does tend to be unreliable and slow. It's better to have mobile data as a backup.

Any mobile data you get will be good throughout Vietnam. Some sellers claim that their sims are only for certain cities — and there were indeed sims like that once upon a time — but nowadays, Vietnamese internet service is nationwide, including even the rural areas.

Censorship

Speaking of Vietnamese internet service: censorship is pretty light. Of major English-language websites, the only major one they block is BBC (because many years ago, BBC dared to run an article about Some People's wealth). They block all the highly political Vietnamese exile groups and news outlets in the US, but I'm assuming you're not reading those, at least not while running around Vietnam. They also block stuff like Human Rights Watch and Freedom House, which is not good for local Vietnamese people, but again, probably not your reading priority on vacation.

But Google, YouTube, Amazon, Gmail, Facebook, TikTok, Instagram, WhatsApp, Line, all the chat services, all the social media sites, and just about everything else works very well. And yes, so do the dating and "dating" apps, including Tinder, Grindr, and all the other -ers.

If you do need to access something "naughty" in Vietnam, just get Tor. Or just try using a free proxy like 1.1.1.1. Some Vietnamese internet blocking can be circumvented by just setting your DNS to something like 8.8.8.8 instead of the one you get from your Vietnamese provider.

Esims

The best option for mobile internet is to get an esim, if your phone supports them. Lots of places online sell them. You can look on Klook — no link, because I don't do referral links. But my recommended place to buy a Vietnam esim is Billion Connect:

https://www.billionconnect.net/

The esims sold on Billion Connect are, in my experience, mega reliable and mega cheap. Figure $10 or less for a ton of data on a two-week sim card.

Note that some of the esims on Billion Connect let you choose the activation date. That activation date is on China time, and that's when your esim will start working. You can install it before then, but it will give you "no service" until the activation date. But if there's no activation date on the purchase page, the esim activates (and the countdown to expiration begins) as soon as you buy it. Not a huge deal financially, because a 30-day sim might cost you a dollar more than a 15-day sim, but just be aware of that esim expiration countdown.

There's also VietnamESim, aka Giga Go (isn't that a man who takes money for — ok never mind):

https://vietnamesim.com/

Physical sims

Physical sim cards with prepaid cellphone service are plentiful and cheap. They cost around 60,000 - 100,000 for a month of service. That's less than five bucks. Almost all cellphone service in Vietnam is prepaid. And while other guidebooks will correctly tell you that Vietnamese law allows sim cards only to be sold from official government stores, I will correctly tell you that this law, like many laws in Vietnam, is completely ignored. Anyone will sell you a sim card. However, bigger stores, in semi-adherence with the law, will record your passport information when you buy a sim card from them.

The two big phone companies are called Mobifone and Vinaphone. They're pretty much identical in terms of prices, policies, and service. Choose whichever.

The thing about sim cards is that it's easy to get cheated and overcharged, because there's no way to check the goods on the spot, unless you're a phone nerd (as most Vietnamese people under 40 are) and can instantly identify the details of the sim card by looking at it. I don't recommend buying a sim card from some dude at the airport or standing on the street soliciting tourists. Those are often used sim cards with only enough credit left on them to give the vendor time to get out of sight.

I strongly recommend that you buy your sim card from the most reliable store that sells them: The Gioi Di Dong (sounds like a mouthful, but it means "world of mobiles," and it's kind of the Best Buy of Vietnam). It's a chain of cellphone stores all over Vietnam. The branch I strongly recommend in Danang—because they are really nice people—is at 351 Nguyen Huu Tho. There's another branch of The Gioi Di Dong at 110 Nguyen Van Linh, near the Dragon Bridge.

Another option is to pre-buy your sim card on Klook, and pick it up at the Danang airport. It costs about $6-$8 for a good sim card with lots of included data. Yes, that's correct, and there's no zero missing. It's like two dollars more expensive than the basic price, but I think the convenience is well worth it. This is a very reliable option. The only difficulty is making sure you can find the Klook desk at the airport. Usually it's right after baggage claim, with a big orange signboard, but they do move around sometimes.

Free wifi

But there's even more good news! (I promise I'm not going to try to convert you to anything, other than maybe cafesuadaism.) Everywhere in Vietnam has free wifi. Absolutely everywhere. Every hotel, every restaurant, every cafe, every store, every gas station, every massage shop, everywhere. Just ask for the password (in Vietnamese password is "mat khau," but you can just say "wifi" and wave your phone and they'll understand). There is also supposed to be free municipal wifi in Danang, although I've never been able to connect to it.

Getting around Danang

Passenger manifests

Transportation providers, such as tour drivers, bus and van drivers, and even taxi drivers, in Danang may ask you to fill out a form with your name, DOB, and citizenship country. Grab should already have this information, but it may not be available to the driver, so on longer trips, Grab drivers may also ask you to write down this information.

The law in Vietnam has for several years specified that the driver of any vehicle needs to have a passenger manifest (seriously) available to show to the police. The law was previously never taken seriously. (Just like the law on seat belts, the law on DUI, the law banning smoking while driving, and on and on.)

But recently the police in Danang, and seemingly only in Danang, have begun using this law for shakedowns. They have been randomly stopping Grab drivers and tour vehicles and demanding their passenger manifests. The fine for not having a manifest is 7 million VND, so it's an easy way for them to collect a bribe of maybe half that from the driver.

You can just write a fake name and info if you want, but I suggest you give truthful info, in case the police moves on to shake you down next if they can't shake down the driver. Foreigners in Vietnam are "required by law" to always carry their original passports, although this is never enforced, especially if you're not ethnically Vietnamese — but I suggest having a photo of your passport on your phone just in case, and your life will be much easier if the info on your passport matches the info on the passenger manifest.

You'll hate me for saying it, but please avoid motorcycles

Traffic in Danang is not nearly as bad as in Saigon or Hanoi. But don't be tempted to rent a motorcycle. It's dangerous and illegal for a foreigner to drive a motorcycle in Vietnam. No matter what the online chatter or the people at the rental place say, your foreign or "international" license is not valid in Vietnam.

As with all laws in Vietnam, you can buy your way out of this law — but that's not the same thing as the law actually allowing it.

Many foreigners do illegally drive motorcycles in Vietnam, you run the risk of jail and five-figure-USD compensation payments (and time in jail, or at least time without your passport, until you cough up the money) should you cause (or be accused of causing) an accident. You are also driving illegally, without a license, and your motorcycle can be confiscated (especially if the cop takes a liking to it) perfectly legally. If it's a rental motorcycle getting confiscated, be prepared for the rental company to claim that it's worth eight trillion dollars, approximately. I've heard unconfirmed rumors of motorcycle rental companies in Vietnam cooperating with the cops on this: the cops get a motorcycle, and the rental company gets a wildly inflated amount of "compensation" (from you!) for the confiscated motorcycle.

Then there's the physical danger. We have sky-high motorcycle fatalities (mostly unreported) in Vietnam. People in cars or trucks don't care about motorcycles on the road, and those roads are full of motor oil, mud, gravel, and other debris. And our "helmets" are close to worthless.

That's not even getting into the more mundane risks of driving a motorcycle in Vietnam, such as having your motorcycle stolen, having parts of it stolen, suffering a mechanical breakdown or flat tire, or getting into a scrape that won't kill you but can make your trip unpleasant and expensive.

Grab Car

But why would you want to rent a motorcycle when getting around by car is so cheap? Grab is the Southeast Asian version of Uber or Lyft. You can enter your destination directly into the Grab Car app and don't need to try to explain it or pronounce it or write it. It's just like Uber in the first world, but much cheaper. Your average ride around town will cost you around 50K VND ($2), and a longer trip out of town might cost you 200K ($8). Going from Danang to Hoi An by car is around 250K-350K, $10-$15, depending on time of day and surge rates and so on.

You should download the Grab app for your Android or Apple phone. You can verify a Grab account using WhatsApp from an international phone number. Unlike the case with Uber, you can't use Grab from a regular computer or web browser or tablet.

Go to the "Subscriptions" section of the Grab app, and try to sign up for any subscription you can find, even if you don't understand what it says (the subscriptions' names are only in Vietnamese).

Here is some outdated info on Grab's website about one of their subscription plans. The actual plans have changed many times since this page was created (and never updated), but this gives you a general idea:

https://www.grab.com/vn/en/grabunlimited/

All the Grab subscriptions will give you big (20-30%) discounts on Grab Car, for some silly cheap amount of money. You will usually need to have a credit card entered into Grab before you can sign up for a subscription. Basically the subscriptions are local pricing — they are meant only for locals who are regular users of Grab. Most Vietnamese users of Grab use it only for special occasions, such as when they have more people they can fit on a motorcycle (five? six?). Those Grab subscriptions are especially important if you plan on taking farther-away trips, such as to Hoi An or Ba Na. Click on Offers in the ride ordering menu to get a list of available discounts.

Note however, that independent of subscriptions, Grab sometimes has discounted fares available in the ride selection menu — it shows up as a different "type" of car, sometimes something like Grab Car Tiet Kiem (Tiet Kiem is savings) or Grab Car Da Nang or something. It's complicated because it's supposed to be complicated.

When booking your Grab Car, you do have to click on the "Offers" button to choose a discount code. Otherwise, no discount for you. For going to popular tourist places, such as Hoi An Old Town and Ba Na Hills, there will often be a discount listed called "Diem Du Lich," giving you 30% off — sometimes only with a subscription, or sometimes even without.

Yes, Grab does offer Grab Bike, their motorcycle taxi service. Yes, it's cheaper than the car service. No, I don't recommend it. It's dangerous, nobody will help you or pay your bills if you're in an accident. The helmet they lend you is not only useless in a crash, but full of head lice, absolutely guaranteed. Don't do it.

By the way, as of 2025, Grab has started charging a 4% surcharge on foreign credit and debit cards. Because it can. You won't see it in the fare quoted, but will see it in your total final bill.

Grab alternatives

Other ways to perish, um I mean travel on Danang's roads? Besides renting a motorcycle, of course. (If you are set on that, almost every hotel in Danang, other than the five-star resorts, will rent you a motorcycle for 150K VND a day.)

There is now a Grab Car competitor called Xanh or Cu Xanh or Xanh Taxi or Xanh SM or Green Taxi. You can download the app. It requires a Vietnamese phone number to verify your account, and the drivers often don't show up. I don't recommend it, because it doesn't give you anything over Grab, over admittedly often newer and comfier cars. But the drivers are super unreliable and don't show up probably more than half the time, and you can't enter a foreign credit card into the app. Vinfast, that famous absolutely totally legitimate electric car company, owns Xanh.

Unlike the case in Saigon, there really aren't many "xe om" (one-man motorcycle taxi companies) hanging around on street corners in Danang.

Anyway, even if you find one, I'm going to warn you not to take them. They're dangerous and they'll charge you whatever they think they can get from you.

Avoid any taxis. There were some honest taxis a decade ago, but now all the honest taxi drivers have gone to Grab. The only drivers still in taxis are either scammers or were fired from Grab — or, of course, both.

Highly recommended *guy*: Mr. Phong

As you may recall from my other guidebooks, I recommend having "a guy" when traveling in Vietnam outside Saigon and Hanoi. This is a driver, guide, and fixer — most importantly, a driver for going longer distances, and especially being available to bring you back from faraway destinations. Sometimes there's no Grab Car available in rural places in Vietnam (not necessarily no Grab Car service, but just no car at that moment in that place). That and it's nice to be able to leave your backpack in the car and so on. And a guy can help you out with tasks that are difficult for a foreigner — for example, figuring out the real price and real ticket booth of an attraction — but trivial for a local Vietnamese person. (And I'd love to, but I'm kind of busy.)

There are many avenues for getting a guy. Many Grab drivers will give you their business card, and a hotel usually can recommend a guy. It's harder to find a guy who speaks English.

I have a trustworthy English-speaking guy to recommend to you. His name is Phong. He's been good to me and my relatives. He speaks English well and has a comfy Toyota Vios (and can rent a bigger car if needed). He's a civil engineer by education. And he's a very good, trustworthy guy and friendly to chat with. He speaks English pretty well, though he doesn't get much practice, so please speak slowly and clearly with him. He can give you cultural insights and be your tour guide if you'd like and so on. He is born and raised in Danang.

Mr. Phong has authorized me to publicize his WhatsApp number: +84 98 246 84 61. Message him in simple, clear, non-slangy English. He can drive you wherever you need around Danang, and I'm sure he'd be willing to discuss longer car trips as well.

In case Mr. Phong is unavailable, I have a backup guy: Mr. Tuan, Whatsapp at +84 90 812 24 67. He's *also* an underemployed engineer. His English is also pretty good. And he's originally from Saigon, so he's obviously an excellent person. I don't know Tuan as well as I know Phong, but he seems trustworthy as far as I can tell.

I have no affiliation with either guy. They don't know that I write guidebooks. And while I recommend them, I don't control them, so please use caution as you'd use dealing with anyone, anywhere.

Walking

For crossing the street, you might have heard the stories about scary street-crossing in Saigon and Hanoi. That doesn't really apply in Danang. The traffic isn't dense enough for it to be too scary. Just wait for an opening in the traffic, and walk (don't run!) your way across, making sure to make eye contact with drivers. You can also raise your hand, especially if you're a physically small person, to make yourself more visible.

The zebra markings on the road — and red and green pedestrian lights — are meaningless and neither pedestrians nor drivers care about them. You don't really have the right of way, and drivers will run you over if you play chicken with them.

Even for cars, red lights and green lights are suggestions. Look both ways always, and remember that motorcycles often drive on the wrong side of the road, or going the wrong way on one-way streets. Remember that if you're injured in an accident, you're not going to be collecting any money from anybody in Vietnam.

Other than the risk of an inglorious death, the walking is great in Danang! Given the time and patience, you can walk anywhere in Danang! Unlike the case in my beloved Saigon, the sidewalks in Danang are sort-of clear for walking. , and the weather usually isn't too hot. You can even walk across the bridges if you want. Theoretically (meaning, if you have the time and energy and it doesn't rain) you could even walk to downtown from the airport. Great stuff!

Geographic overview, and where to stay in Danang

Danang is bisected north-south by the Han River, and the river is famously crossed east-west by Danang's five bridges. We can call the part of Danang west of the river the city area, and the part of Danang east of the river the beach area. Until the new bridges were built—the most significant one, the Dragon Bridge, only in 2013—the beach side was the poor boondocks of Danang where nobody wanted to go.

More precisely and legalistically, Danang is geographically divided into eight quans. Each quan (pronounced *gwan*) is a neighborhood. The main two quans you should at least recognize the names of are Hai Chau, which is most of city-side urban Danang (west side, what's up), and Son Tra, which is most of beach-side Danang (east side, what's up). There's also Thanh Ke, which encompasses the beachside northwest corner of urban Danang, and Ngu Hanh Son, the southernmost part of beach-side Danang. I love Thanh Ke, but Ngu Hanh Son won't be on the test, because there's still not much there.

East side or west side?

The beach side (east side) is quite long north-to-south. The south part of that beach side is known as the American/Australian/European expat area, with quite a few English-language and foreigner-oriented establishments on the small streets. The north part of the beach side is dominated by hotels for Korean tourists, and new construction of more hotels for Korean tourists. The middle, near the Dragon Bridge, is the closest that the beach side has to a downtown; it's also the part that has Son Tra Night Market. You might even be able to find an open cafe in this part of the beach side if you're there between the hours of 1:07 P.M. and 1:09 P.M. every third Wednesday. (Am I too harsh on beach-side Danang?)

I strongly suggest you open Google Maps and take a look at Danang, and maybe even look on Google Maps as you read this book and see the places I recommend. That will give you a good idea of the city.

Danang trivia: Hoang Sa, known in English as the Paracel Islands, is (according to Vietnamese policy and law, not according to daily usage) a quan of Danang. Someone please tell that to the thousands of Chinese soldiers stationed there. Um, I'll wait right here while you do that.

Should you stay on the east side or west side of Danang? Here's the thing about the east side: it's generally just you and the beach. The east side is very undeveloped. What there is on the east side is all for tourists. It's pretty distant from an authentic Vietnamese or Danang experience. Stay on the east side only if you are consciously trying to get away from the world and have nothing nearby but foreign tourists and the beach.

That can be good if you want the feeling of an unspoiled beachside retreat, or bad if you want to buy a bottle of water or a cup of coffee. There aren't even many convenience stores on the east side; you just have to find a grandma on a corner who's selling what you need, or eat in your hotel, if your hotel has food.

As you might have expected though, the beach side is generally favored by tourists and expats, especially American and European expats—and the "undeveloped" beach side is where you'll find a lot of tourist-oriented businesses. Also perhaps unexpectedly, the beach side tends to be a bit cheaper for hotels, at least when we're talking about modest family hotels, not beach resorts.

You could live on the urban west side and take a taxi to the east side for less than 100,000 VND one-way whenever you want to go to the beach. But I think many people just want to passively be in a beach and oceanfront environment, and wouldn't specifically take a taxi to the beach. (That and for about half the year, Danang's beaches are too cold for swimming.) Or you could live on the east side and take a taxi or car to the west side whenever you want to eat anything or buy anything or use electricity. (Just kidding on the last one. Or am I?). The problem with either version of that plan is that you rack up a lot of cross-bridge trips and Grab or taxi fares, and taxis are pretty scarce on the east side at night.

So I don't know. Decide how important it is for you to be near the oceanfront. If you're willing to put up with inconvenience to be near the beaches, go for it. If you'd rather be able to walk out of your hotel and find a convenience store and whatever else you need, stay on the west side. The west side is also much closer to just about everything, including the airport.

A dark horse candidate: Thanh Khe

Beach side or west side? West side or beach side?

Porque no los dos?

Why not both?

Foreign tourists consider the beach to consist entirely of the east side of Danang. But there's an underappreciated and very local stretch of beach on the west side: Thanh Khe. North of the central city, it's the Danang beach most popular with Vietnamese tourists, and with Danang locals.

As far as the actual water and the beach, Thanh Khe is no worse than any beach on the east side. What it does lack is the feeling of rustic faraway seclusion of the east side. In Thanh Khe, you'll get your beautiful beach, but in the background of your Insta, you might have not lush jungle but a busy road and a gas station and a cafe — you know, Vietnam!

Being close to urban life also means being close to urban life. Conveniences. Restaurants. Cafes. Grab Cars. Population. Civilization. Electrification.

A lot of Thanh Khe is really aimed at Vietnamese tourists, and what those Vietnamese tourists associate with the beach: mostly boozing and seafood. You can use that to your advantage.

Example: there's a wonderful *goi ca*, Vietnamese raw fish salad rolls (sort of Vietnamese sushi rolls), restaurant in Thanh Khe, called Be Van (Baby Van). https://maps.app.goo.gl/woQ6ocTq4mb8GJbz6

Random foreigners walk in to Be Van and order pho or banh mi and walk out of there thinking that restaurant is no good. But if they just knew that this part of town is all about the seafood, and you're supposed to order sushi rolls (goi ca) here, and that ordering pho here is about the same as ordering sushi in a pho restaurant — foreign tourists don't get the best of Thanh Khe, is what I'm saying.

One nice gentle introduction to Thanh Khe can be Amazing Beach Bar, a very foreigner-friendly and English-friendly bar right on the beach in Thanh Khe:

https://maps.app.goo.gl/U5raEZwJrCRVigxt7

We'll talk about Thanh Khe in this book. It's going a bit of a transformation nowadays, starting to try to attract foreigners. I'm all in on that effort, and will try to entice you to consider Thanh Khe as well. It's a good way to be simultaneously close to the beach and to the city center. The downside is that Thanh Khe can be kind of gritty, and the English isn't so great out there. But this is Vietnam, isn't it? Not-so-great English should be your indicator that you're going where not many foreigners have tread before you.

Hotel recommendations

Prices

The good news in Danang is that wherever you stay, cheap hotel rooms are plentiful. How cheap? You can easily find a totally livable room—yes, with wifi, daily maid cleaning, and none of the indignities of a hostel—for under $20 a night. In fact, I've seen the inside of both the cheaper and the more expensive hotels in Danang, and I really don't think there's much of a difference in the rooms: in the more expensive hotels all you're paying for is English-speaking employees, and of course marketing.

Once I went to Danang to meet up with some relatives of mine from the US who had booked a room at one of the expensive beachfront hotels. I didn't want to be homeless Elly on the sofa in their hotel room—although they did offer—so I booked myself a room at a cheap small hotel down the street from their expensive hotel. My hotel cost $20 a night. Their hotel cost $150 a night. The rooms were identical. The only difference was their hotel was a taller building, and the staff at their hotel spoke better English.

As is the case everywhere in Vietnam, there is a huge price premium for hotels with internationally recognizable chain names. The international chains know that, and are moving in. There are now Hiltons, Sheratons, Hyatts, and just about all the major brands in Danang, even on the west side.

While I know brands from home are comforting, if you're shopping on the higher end of hotel rooms in Danang, don't stay in an international chain hotel unless you want to pay about double of what you'd pay at a non-chain hotel for exactly the same room. (My estimate of "double" isn't something out of thin air: international chain hotels in Vietnam have to be 51%-49% "joint ventures" with you-know-who, and therefore have to hand over 51% of their income to you-know-who.)

As counterintuitive as it is, try to stay with hotel brands that aren't familiar to you from back in your country. You'll get much more for your money that way.

Here's the secret (not really secret, but seldom known outside Southeast Asia) site to book hotels in Danang or anywhere else in Vietnam:

http://agoda.com Agoda, unlike most US-based booking sites, has a strong local Vietnamese presence, and they're good at signing up small local hotels that may not have any English-speaking staff to deal with companies like Expedia. Agoda also has an app.

You will find tons and tons of small local hotels on Agoda that don't show up on Expedia, Orbitz, or any of the big US-based sites. And the hotels that do show up on Expedia tend to be much more expensive there than on Agoda.

The downside of Agoda? Don't expect customer service, or any kind of service. Don't expect "the customer is always right." Don't expect to even be able to contact them to tell them about your problems. And most frustratingly, Agoda allows your hotel to cancel your reservation when it feels like it, generally when you reserved at a low price and there's a surge in demand so they can get more for that room — they'll just cancel your reservation and send you a short email saying your reservation is canceled. Ask me how I know!

What recourse do you have in Vietnam? None. Unless you have an uncle who can send some guys around.

That's also why I don't recommend Airbnb type arrangements in Vietnam. There is so much scamming at so many different levels, and in Vietnam, consumers have no recourse. Yes, Airbnb will eventually give you a refund (maybe), but what good is that when your vacation was ruined? (Do I sound like a hotel ad yet?) That and I don't think many first-worlders would be happy living in a Vietnamese highrise condo building, which is the usual Airbnb arrangement. Imagine 3 AM karaoke, cigarette stench everywhere, water outages or leakages, and on and on.

Yes, there are hostels in Danang. No, I don't see the point. When a nice hotel room costs $15, why would you pay $10 for a bunk bed with a bunch of gross smelly people who might steal your stuff?

I couldn't stay in most hostels in Vietnam anyway, because hostels in Vietnam usually bar Vietnamese people from staying there — because we're all thieves and drug dealers. That's ok; I didn't want to stay in your ratty hostel anyway. Back to the hotel talk then.

In my opinion, the sweet spot for hotels in Danang is around $20-$50 per night. I think if you pay more than that, you won't get much more. If you pay less than that, you might get a place that's a bit cramped or a building that's a bit run-down.

I'll give you a few specific ideas for hotels in Danang. These are just hotels I'm familiar with from my Danang wanderings and research and that I know of as being generally well regarded. I've even stayed in most of them. I mean this list as a starting point. There are lots and lots of hotels in Danang, and many great hotels I've never heard of, not to mention never reviewed. Check out the reviews on Google or Tripadvisor (warning: Agoda reviews are basically fake; they only publish the reviews they choose to publish, which are the most positive ones) and go for it. My list is meant to get you started researching, not to be an exhaustive list.

Each hotel is followed by an approximate nightly price for an average room during an average season. I don't own any of these hotels, so I can't guarantee that these prices will stay the same. Also, while I've personally visited all these hotels and stayed in some of them, I can't guarantee that they'll be exactly what you want, so please check Tripadvisor or other rating sites. As always, I strongly recommend you book any hotel in Vietnam on Agoda and use your credit card or Paypal to pay.

Ten specific hotel recommendations

Here are ten specific hotels I recommend you consider. While these are all good places, there are tons of other good places in Danang, so please use this as a starting point.

The prices I'm giving here are very rough estimates, obviously — I usually avoid traveling during any sort of high season, so the prices I'm familiar with are probably on the low end of what you'll experience. Remember to book on Agoda, which has the best prices and worst service.

Mitisa (Hai Chau, $30)

https://maps.app.goo.gl/JQDLAMgwes1tBqLU7[1]

---

1. https://maps.app.goo.gl/JQDLAMgwes1tBqLU7

This is where I usually stay. I love the Mitisa Hotel on the city side for a good combination of everything, an amazing location (right at the Dragon Bridge), good service, and a good price. The service is pretty good as well, and the maids do a great job — I kind of have a jones for my room being cleaned very thoroughly every morning.

There's a convenience store (tap hoa, not a real convenience store) on one side of the hotel, and a Phuc Long Cafe on the other side. There are some hip cafes down the road, and the HSBC ATM is like a five-minute walk away, and the food street (Huynh Thuc Khang) is only a ten minute walk. Plus you can see (and easily walk to) the Dragon Bridge. It's great. But please don't automatically stay at Mitisa just because I do. There are tons of great hotels in Danang, and your tastes might differ from mine.

Jim's House (Hai Chau, $20)

https://maps.app.goo.gl/243keFdxu4mLU2SA9[2]

Jim's House has very much a hostel vibe, even if the rooms and bathrooms are private. There's a rooftop garden and hangout area, going along with the social hostel vibe. But the most important feature of Jim's House is the location: it's on Danang's greatest food street, Huynh Thuc Khang. You'll get fat. That's a feature, not a bug.

---

2. https://maps.app.goo.gl/243keFdxu4mLU2SA9

Minh Toan Galaxy (Hai Chau, $30)

https://maps.app.goo.gl/zNGAkUHbPAcRinN87[3]

I have a soft spot for the Minh Toan Galaxy on the city side. The Minh Toan Galaxy is a big, old building, from Vietnam's hardline communist days, although it has been recently renovated. I think it's a bit of urban Vietnamese history. I like that kind of stuff. Also, it's right next to the weird defunct Danang Downtown Sunworld Whatever amusement park.

Binh Duong (Hai Chau, $15)

https://maps.app.goo.gl/uMiATwVDSCf8YdwYA[4]

Binh Duong used to be a Vietnamese army dorm/guesthouse. Then it became an upscale hotel. And now it's a pretty down-at-the-heels hotel. But for the price, it's surprisingly good. From the exterior, you could mistake it for a fancy four-star hotel. It's not. But you could mistake it for one, from the outside and even the lobby.

It has big rooms and hot water and only occasional all-night meth parties. Yes, the crowd is a bit sketchy, but I don't think they'll bother foreigners. But don't expect the cream of society staying here. And definitely don't expect no-smoking, no matter what the signs say. Still, it's a solid and comfy place, and I love the vintage communist vibe, which also permeates the neighborhood.

---

3. https://maps.app.goo.gl/zNGAkUHbPAcRinN87

4. https://maps.app.goo.gl/uMiATwVDSCf8YdwYA

The Binh Duong is pretty much next door to a bunch of really cool vintage cafes, as well as to the public library.

Let's be clear: I don't recommend staying at the Binh Duong if you can afford a better place. Don't complain to me that I "recommended" this sketchy hotel to you. I'm recommending it only if all you've got to your name is $15 a night, and in that case, the Binh Duong is a great option.

Santori (Thanh Khe, $25)

https://maps.app.goo.gl/XmX2e6ZiGPh6KhG38[5]

This is a cute blue-and-white hotel right on the beach (well, across the road from the beach) in the previously mentioned underrated urban beach district north of the central city, Thanh Khe. It's supposedly inspired by Santorini, Greece, which is a popular Vietnamese decor trope. Lots of beach views. There's even a swimming pool. And it's right next to my recommended raw fish restaurant and beach bar in Thanh Khe. All that for $25. The downside is that yes, before the beach, there's a somewhat busy road right in front of you, but that's sort of the charm of Thanh Khe. Besides the road, it's also near the airport, and all the Jeju Air flights will take off directly overhead. Not so many though. Just relax at the pool and pretend you're one of those beachside-airplane-watchers in St. Maarten.

Avenis (Thanh Khe, $25)

https://maps.app.goo.gl/WLs6DwAni7bpcCoKA[6]

---

5. https://maps.app.goo.gl/XmX2e6ZiGPh6KhG38

6. https://maps.app.goo.gl/WLs6DwAni7bpcCoKA

Avenis is a great deal: right on the beach in Thanh Khe, big rooms, rooftop terrace (with a tiny bathtub-sized "swimming pool"), all for around $25. It's a bit farther from the central city than Santori — that could be good or bad. It's definitely quieter than Santori. The decor and exterior appearance are just your regular bland off-white Vietnamese hotel standard, not the Santori's blue-and-white cuteness. It's not on the flight path. And thanks to being farther from the central city, the road between the hotel and the beach isn't busy.

Sunflower (Phuoc My, $10)

https://maps.app.goo.gl/sMicHhPoScyoqjV1A[7]

Sunflower is a pretty great bargain on the north part of the beach side. I've stayed there when once attempting to do the cheapest Danang trip possible. It's a $10 hotel room that really isn't too bad and doesn't feel like a "$10 hotel room." It's kind of in the middle of a bunch of empty lots and construction sites with not much nearby, other than Wind Garden Cafe — and the beach! The beach is of course just a short walk away. The employees are pretty good with their English. Note that Sunflower, like most hotels in Vietnam, does shady stuff to get five-star Google reviews, so don't trust all the reviews, but this is a good hotel anyway.

Yarra (Ngu Hanh Son, $30)

https://maps.app.goo.gl/NkHLBhMqTjCQgwkF7[8]

---

7. https://maps.app.goo.gl/sMicHhPoScyoqjV1A

Yarra is value, value, value. It's a very comfy new hotel in a tall building, with a rooftop pool. It's right on the beach on the east side. And it only costs around $30. It gets some bad reviews online because it calls itself a four-star hotel, and first-worlders show up expecting a real four-star hotel. This is Vietnam. Don't expect perfect service, absolute cleanliness, and so on, in a $30 hotel in Vietnam, even if it calls itself four-star. But if your expectations are realistic, Yarra is a wonderful place for a beach getaway. It's in Ngu Hanh Son, away from civilization, but that's kind of the point.

Furama (Ngu Hanh Son, $200)

https://maps.app.goo.gl/t3oFAzmUxYiTdoDt8[9]

Furama is the beach side's value-for-money luxury resort option. It is an honest-to-goodness four-star resort. At Furama, you (probably) won't find the sleeping front desk clerks, leaking shower heads, and lingering cigarette smoke smells of the $30 "four-star" hotels I've recommended here. Of course, $200 a night (about 5 million VND) is a month's blue-collar pay in Vietnam, so I'm not sure how much of a good deal it can be at this price. Still, it's cheaper than the international brand places, and not any worse.

Olalani (Ngu Hanh Son, $70)

https://maps.app.goo.gl/va5WEDsELBFWFhdX8[10]

---

8. https://maps.app.goo.gl/NkHLBhMqTjCQgwkF7

9. https://maps.app.goo.gl/t3oFAzmUxYiTdoDt8

What the Furama is to the four-star-resort space, Olalani is to the two-and-a-half or generously three-star resort space. It's a place for the Vietnamese — mostly Saigonese — upper middle class to take a family vacation. There's a little bit of the jankiness you'll find in a regular Vietnamese hotel, but the beach is unbeatable, and the facilities are pretty nice.

Final hotel notes

The northern beach-side hotels are focused on Korean tourists. They may not really speak English, even if they're focused on international tourists, because almost all their tourists are Korean. Meanwhile, the hotels on the south side of the beach side are focused on European, American, and Australian (read: white) tourists, especially those interested in surfing. The north of the beach side is more populated and "developed" than the south.

Beach side hotels will generally speak more English (or at least Korean), because city side hotels encounter few foreigners.

The beach-side resorts, most prominently the Furama and the Hyatt, are focused on you staying there at the resort and not really venturing outside. They're pretty far from everything else (though the Furama is less far than the Hyatt). I would recommend those if you want to "get away from it all," but less so if you want to be experiencing Danang every day. Some of the beach side hotels won't even let you get food delivery, supposedly because of "covid." I didn't know revenue protection is called covid!

Even the cheapest hotels in Vietnam have free wifi, hot water, towels, clean bathrooms, toiletries, and toothpaste and toothbrushes. I can't promise that you'll get the finest-quality toiletries or that the internet will be fast enough to let you stream Pokimane, but anyway, those amenities will be there, and they'll be of passable quality and free of charge even if your hotel costs only $10 a

---

10. https://maps.app.goo.gl/va5WEDsELBFWFhdX8

night. I've never heard of a hotel in Vietnam that doesn't have free wifi (at least not in the past decade).

Next-to-last point: Often the cheapest rooms in any Vietnamese hotel will be windowless. Make sure your room has a window. Its listing on Agoda should specifically mention it. If a window or view is not mentioned, assume there's no window.

Last point: Hotels in Vietnam, unlike hotels in most of the rest of the world, charge different prices based on how many people are in the room. So while I know that when you book hotel rooms in the US you don't have to tell them in advance how many people will be in the room (as long as it's a reasonable number), in Vietnam, there's a per-person charge. So make sure your Agoda reservation has the correct number of people. Otherwise, when you check in, the front desk will demand a cash payment that will in all likelihood be much more expensive than the price differential you would've paid on Agoda for reserving with the correct number of people in the room. Hey, hotel desk clerks have to buy gas for their motorcycles too!

Cafes aren't just for coffee

That sounds salacious. Wink wink nudge nudge. But that's not what I mean. What I mean is that in Vietnamese culture, cafes aren't where you pop in to have a quick coffee. Cafes are where you relax, socialize, read, work, nap, gossip, meet your friends, get scolded by your parents, make friends, make enemies, fall in love, get dumped, eat dinner, download pirated movies, and floss your teeth. I'm exaggerating only slightly.

In Danang, relatively cheap rent—compared to Hanoi and Saigon, anyway—makes for a wealth of cafes and cafe entrepreneurs. "I want to start a cafe in Danang" is nowadays kind of a common dream for young people in Saigon, generally young people who couldn't afford to start a cafe in Saigon, but find it much more realistic in Danang. Danang is full of emigres from Hanoi and Saigon starting new businesses. And, you guessed it, as with most things in Danang, the only way to find these places is word of mouth.

In all of the cafes I'm listing here, you'll find free wifi, and in all but SixOnSix (which is not really Vietnamese), you'll get free water or iced tea. Expect to pay anywhere from around 20,000 to around 80,000 for a coffee drink — of course what you're really paying for is the real estate of a place to sit all day, use the wifi and the bathroom, drink free iced tea, and bask in the air conditioning.

All but the last two cafes are on the city side. The last two are on the beach side: Six On Six on the southern beach side and Wind Garden on the northern beach side.

Long Coffee

123 Le Loi, Hai Chau
    https://maps.app.goo.gl/oWZKKogafAESmYfZ9

Drinks 15K-20K

If you were Vietnamese (and maybe you are), Long Coffee would be where your grandpa goes in the morning to meet his buddies, smoke a pack of cigarettes, play dominoes, and complain about his grandkids. When he was young, they didn't drink all these fancy lattes, and people knew that smoking is good for you. So that's the kind of place Long Cafe is. Expect an older crowd, although now young Vietnamese hipsters are kind of into this place in a retro way, maybe the same way American hipsters are into dive bars. Expect lots of cigarette smoke. Expect older gentlemen with questionable hearing speaking not-very-quietly. It's part of the charm. You can have any kind of coffee you want, kiddo, as long as it's hot or cold (nong or da), with or without milk (sua or den). They all cost 20K or less anyway. Yes, that's under a buck. Sit on hard wooden stools and watch the street, because of course. Note that the official closing time is 7 PM, but that's just when they literally close the doors; last order is 6 PM, and they kick you out around 6:45 PM. Ask me how I know!

Noi Cafe

Three shops in the alley at 113 Nguyen Chi Thanh, Hai Chau
    https://maps.app.goo.gl/bp5xz3eXhq8kxamy7

Drinks 30K-50K

Can't you just pick one location?! No, no they can't. It's hilarious and wonderful how Noi has three "branches," all in the same alley — basically old shop spaces they've bought out and turned into their own vintage style cafe. They're all super comfy and riffs on the same theme, with the same menu, but each one in a slightly different space. You'll see what I mean. The service is pretty good, and you can sit on old-style hard wooden chairs, or on folding "camping chairs." Not very laptop-comfy. Lots of blended fruit drinks, which are pretty great. Unfortunately, because all of these places are open-air (under a roof, but air kind of blowing through), there is no A/C, and there is a lot of cigarette smoking. The good part, though is all the awesome vintage electronics they have sitting around all three spaces.

Khe

In an alley on Tran Phu, near Noi; see Google Maps QR code
    Drinks: 20-30K
    https://maps.app.goo.gl/bKkrVfTnJ8ZWaVZp8

Khe is the alternative to the much more popular Noi, which is just around the corner. It's cheaper, cozier, and most importantly, quieter and less-smokier than Noi. It's actually kind of frighteningly cheap: think 20K drinks for a hipster shop in Hai Chau. Maybe Saigon has whatever-is-the-opposite-of-spoiled me, but at these prices, I'm worried about my kidneys stolen. That hasn't happened. Khe is great. And they do have an English menu.

Local Beans

186 Phan Chau Trinh, Hai Chau

    https://maps.app.goo.gl/ogstrx1nXfHLV9op9

Local Beans, near the Dragon Bridge, is my top recommendation for a working cafe. It's a big and comfy multi-floor space, even if a bit boring. The chairs and tables are set up well for working. Drinks are decent. The staff speaks English. The wifi is reasonably ok, and not password protected. Try the salt cocoa. Local Beans is a Danang copy of Saigon coffee chain Running Bean.

Hoai Niem / Retrospective

121 Huynh Thuc Khang, Hai Chau

https://maps.app.goo.gl/Wx1mtPwgkgQMmrNx7

Hoai niem is a Vietnamese (and Cantonese) term better translated as *nostalgia*. But yeah, *retrospective* is close enough. The great thing about Hoai Niem is it's on the major food street, so you can come here and digest. Sit on folding chairs and watch the street. It's one of those no-AC, open-air places, with the obligatory vintage electronics sitting around. Unfortunately, I get a weird unfriendly vibe from the management, but maybe they just don't like me.

Nam House Coffee

In the alley at 15 Le Hong Phong, Hai Chau
https://maps.app.goo.gl/wT5zR7CoM2Wm2LLWA

Wifi password: 15lehongphong
Drinks 30K-50K
Nam is an awesome imitation of an old-fashioned Vietnamese cafe. Ok, their vintage decor is not really from the 1970s or whatever it's supposed to be from. But despite being fake-vintage, they create an amazing atmosphere. The sign above the entrance says in Vietnamese "This here is Vietnam." True!

Expect only traditional Vietnamese coffee drinks. You can sit in these great big old wooden chairs. Vintage music. Very nice staff. Just a totally relaxing place.

Note that it's hidden down an alley. The Google Maps location is correct, even though when you follow it, you might think it's wrong, because you'll really be going down a small dark alley where you'd never expect a pretty big coffeeshop to be hidden away. But there it is.

Note that there's no address for the cafe specifically. The official address is "near 15 Le Hong Phong," so you'll have to go by that and explore that alley, and just use Google Maps to direct you. The new complementing the old; what could be better?

Phe La and Katinat

35 and 9 Nguyen Van Linh, Hai Chau
   https://maps.app.goo.gl/6FZyaTqJebrmf5Jy8

Drinks 30-60K

I'm being snarky and listing these as one item, because while Phe La and Katinat are independent shops, they're basically the same thing. They're next to each other (with P Coffee between them) on Nguyen Van Linh. They are more about socializing and seeing and being seen, and watching the street, than about the drinks themselves. They're a great way to experience Vietnamese Gen Z life — just don't expect excellent drinks, nor even what you might think of as "Vietnamese coffee." The specialty at both places is sugary nouveau drinks. And don't forget that both have a view of the Dragon Bridge, if you crane your neck to the right enough.

Phe La is a bit more into the "pure coffee" experience, with nitro cold brews and siphon coffees, while Katinat is more into the fruit-flavored "milk tea" (without any tea) side of things — roughly speaking, in the highly gendered Vietnamese cafe scene, those are male and female targeted cafes. No matter what your gender, these places are almost exclusively peopled by the high school and college-age crowd, plus some foreign tourists who look either bemused or terrified.

The Books Garden

46 Bach Dang, Hai Chau

https://maps.app.goo.gl/9sF96LLqvfJVAhyJ6

Drinks 80K

This place is not so much about books as it is about the river view, and the nice shaded patio-garden from which you can enjoy it. It's on Bach Dang, which is the riverside street near Dragon Bridge. Prices are about Saigon level, which is expensive for Danang. There are also some pretty good simple meals, such as *banh mi* sandwiches and *my quang* noodles.

Les 3000 Mondes

121/39 Nguyen Chi Thanh (#39 in the alley at 121 Nguyen Chi Thanh)
https://maps.app.goo.gl/ao7LaaDvJCJ8kty5A

Drinks 50K

I'm not sure whether there's a sly pun in the shop's name. Yes, it's French, but *les* is Vietnamese slang for lesbians. Whatever. The point is, this is Danang's first and only cottagecore cafe. Jane Austen type stuff. It's mostly for what's called "check-in" in Vietglish: social media posting. It's still fun. The audience is, of course, mostly young women. And the drinks and pastries aren't really the point of the place; they're just about acceptable.

Powerhouse

89 Nguyen Thai Hoc, Hai Chau
https://maps.app.goo.gl/ZKHNBBf7VmXpVsBc8

Drinks 50K

This place overlooks the new Danang theater. And, little-known trivia: the building was actually the old Danang theater. Some of the interior decoration nods to that: there are weird vintage (maybe fake?) theater spotlights sitting around, and the exterior has that "fish scale" design popular among Vietnamese communist-brutalist buildings back in the day. It's a big, comfy, multi-level cafe that is great for working. The only downside is that despite the entire cafe being "non-smoking," the upper floors are full of smokers, and the employees don't care (since some of them are smoking too). That's your reminder that we're in Vietnam.

Memory Lounge

7 Bach Dang, Hai Chau, on the waterfront
https://maps.app.goo.gl/PSAcVRYR3zfUt7xC9

Drinks 100K

Memory Lounge is a fancy cafe-lounge right on the riverfront, across the street from the Hilton Hotel. The drinks and coffee are mediocre, but the atmosphere and the view are excellent. Count your change though, because the cashier once tried to cheat me on my change (she "accidentally forgot" to include a 100K bill I was owed in my change), and according to the reviews, I'm not the only victim.

Highlands VTV8

258 Bach Dang, Hai Chau, the glass UFO inside the VTV8 TV station complex

https://maps.app.goo.gl/6TUMK23vFw4K33Sq9

Drinks 30K

This is just another Highlands: cheap, barely acceptable coffee from a Vietnamese coffee chain that makes *cheap, barely acceptable* their brand. But this location is special. It's inside this glass UFO looking structure on the campus of VTV8, Danang's official government-run (there are no other kinds in Vietnam) station. The structure was previously something else, though I don't know what, and you can definitely see how it drips with Vietnamese Communist-brutalist history. It's pretty cool. Unfortunately the all-around glass reflects sound and this place gets loud in the evenings.

Cafe Muoi Hue

254 Tran Phu, Hai Chau

https://maps.app.goo.gl/TiJSxCprbucQpbst8

Wifi password: 254tranphu
Drinks 40-60K

Salted coffee is the hot new thing now in Danang. Muoi means salted. And this place specializes in, yes, salted coffee. Everything on the menu with "muoi" in the name is salted. Salt is supposed to enhance the taste of coffee. Maybe it does. It's definitely an interesting taste, and the coffee itself they brew is excellent. I felt super thirsty afterward, but what else can I expect after drinking coffee and salt?

You'll sit at small wooden chairs and tables outside. Unfortunately, they allow smoking, but when I've been there, not many people were smoking. The crowd is mostly teenagers and college students.

Note that this place is so fashionable that there are tons of imitators with similar or even identical names, both in Google Maps and in the Grab app map. Some of the fakes claim to be branches of the real one; they're not. You're free to try those imitators, but the real shop is at 254 Tran Phu. (By the way, it's very close to Nam Coffee, so you can easily walk between the two.)

La Bonne Cafe

192 Phan Chau Trinh, Hai Chau

https://maps.app.goo.gl/dPGK8zv9nwVkuZLv9

Wifi password: labonnecamon

Drinks 30K-60K

This is a beautiful cafe **WITH CATS** in a big house looking out on the central Hai Chau area and Dragon Bridge, **WITH CATS**. You can chill here all day **WITH CATS**. Drinks aren't great, but who cares, **WITH CATS**.

P Coffee

55 Nguyen Van Linh, Hai Chau

https://maps.app.goo.gl/bNSFsTgCTishciS56

https://www.instagram.com/pcoffee.dn/ (because of course)
Drinks 60K-90K

I can't decide whether this is a beautiful minimalist space and the hippest thing going in Da Nang, or a cynical attempt to pander to the perceived desires of Instagramming young women. Maybe it's both. It's on the same stretch of Nguyen Van Linh as Katinat and Phe La. It's a see-and-be-seen cafe, and it's also all about the Instagram angles. Stark white walls and decorations you want to pose next to. Lots of young women in tight dresses taking selfies and hoping to snag an influencer contract or a rich husband or both. Am I just bitter because I wear yoga pants and running shoes? Maybe. The seats are super-uncomfortable hard wooden stools, probably intentionally so you don't stay too long. The drinks are bad but nobody cares.

TiPi Cafe

57 Pham Van Nghi, Thanh Khe
   https://maps.app.goo.gl/P5XcZnmpZaQ15Fn49

https://www.facebook.com/tipicafe/
Drinks 40K, plus surcharge for Vietnamese people

TiPi is an English-speaking cafe. Not only do the employees speak English, but speaking English is the purpose of the cafe. It's a place to practice English in the evenings, primarily for Vietnamese college students, young working people, and families. It's an easy way to start a conversation about Danang with some local Danang people. They can give you recommendations, tell you stuff about their city, teach you Vietnamese, whatever. They'll be glad to talk with you just to improve their English. Maybe you can make long-term friends there too. Note that TiPi (the name is because it's built like a "teepee"—I guess nobody told them about TP meaning toilet paper) is open only in the evenings, starting around (yup, there's "around" again) 5 PM. Most evenings they have a game show or open mic night or some such thing.

I do have some misgivings about this place. They charge Vietnamese people a 50K VND surcharge for "learning English." Yes, everyone complains about double pricing that charges foreigners more, but this place charges non-foreigners more. Does that mean that they're making money from the unpaid foreigners there? (Not to mention the ridiculous idea that anyone Vietnamese speaks worse English than anyone non-Vietnamese.)

And I assure you that I speak better English than the Vietnamese employees there—and maybe better English than some of the sketchy-looking foreigners there as well—but they charged me the "learning English" surcharge anyway, because I'm Vietnamese. Yes, I'm salty. And none of this will apply to you. Unless you're Vietnamese too. Last word of warning: as in any "forced conversational interaction" event with strangers anywhere in the world, watch out for scammers and Amway recruiters!

SixOnSix Cafe

64 Ba Huyen Thanh Quan, Ngu Hanh Son
   https://maps.app.goo.gl/7fU6Adh5gGKTitAK6

Drinks 70K

This is a living room in an Australian expat's house in Ngu Hanh Son, one of the southern beach-side expat neighborhoods. They speak fluent English and they have big, comfortable sofas, good wifi, and foreigner-friendly food and drinks like lattes and breakfast burritos. Almost all the customers are white foreigners, although Vietnamese hipsters (like me) do like to come here to show off how worldly they are. Everything is in English. Prices are really high. That breakfast burrito will cost you 140,000 VND. Coffee will cost you 50,000 VND. But if you sit there all day, maybe that's not so bad.

Wind Garden Cafe

72 Le Manh Trinh, Phuoc My
https://maps.app.goo.gl/HJ3Z4WG4PerUkCQD8

Drinks 40K

Wind Garden is hidden on a small residential street in an otherwise very, very quiet neighborhood on the north end of the beach side. I actually don't know why Vietnamese people regard this cafe so highly. Yes, it does have a small pond and garden, but it's very, very small, not anything really special, at least not by Saigon standards. The "pond" is the size of, say, an indoor pond in a hotel lobby. I wouldn't make a special trip to go there, but if you're on the beach side, there's not much else around. Drinks are decent and the employees are nice. And when you're looking for the place, you're really not going to believe there's a cafe there, because it's on this very quiet residential street that's kind of in the middle of nowhere near the beach—but yes, there's a cafe there.

Waterfront sugar fix

The waterfront area on the city side near Dragon Bridge has become a haven for dessert shops. Actually, when I wrote this book's first edition, there were a bunch of coconut ice cream shops on the waterfront. Those have faded away (some still taking their last gasps) — and now there's a huge boom of all kinds of much fancier, much less Vietnamese (sad face) dessert options near the city side waterfront. Note that unless otherwise noted, they don't have waterfront views.

Dua Ben Tre 190

https://maps.app.goo.gl/BhCmtPqXFPtVTX5Y7[1]

Dua Ben Tre 190, at 190 Bach Dang, is the granddaddy that started it all: the oldest still-enduring coconut dessert shop on the waterfront. It does actually have a waterfront view. And they specialize in all kinds of coconut desserts: coconut ice cream, jelly, puddings, milk tea, yogurt, and anything else you can think of. Yes, the menu has (somewhat questionable) English. Prices are cheap, like under 50K. By the way, Ben Tre is the province southwest of Saigon that's closely associated with coconut-growing. *Bach Dang*, the street name, means *pier*. And there's a very similar coconut dessert place a couple of doors away, at 198 Bach Dang; same idea.

Kem Dua Ma Lai

https://maps.app.goo.gl/96mKtDuV1F5mZHhL8[2]

---

1. https://maps.app.goo.gl/BhCmtPqXFPtVTX5Y7

2. https://maps.app.goo.gl/96mKtDuV1F5mZHhL8

The name means *Malaysian Coconut Ice Cream*. I don't know whether it's Malaysian, but it definitely is great. And the people working here are super-nice. And the prices are cheap: I think an ice cream cone is 15K or something. The worst thing I can say about this place is on weekend evenings it's super-crowded with the high school crowd.

Cloudy Nitrogen Ice Cream

https://maps.app.goo.gl/WggqrtLMQkxtrxmt6[3]

Besides the usual milk tea (sweetened/flavored milk, really), they specialize in "nitrogen" ice cream. While there's a trend of the heaviest, fattiest ice cream, there's an opposite trend of "nitrogen" ice cream, which is made lighter and airier by a carbonation-like process. So Cloudy specializes in nitrogen ice cream. Try the milk tea (Oreo) cookie ice cream flavor.

The location is full of teenagers hanging out, especially in the evenings. If you were Vietnamese, you'd be considered weird for going here when you're over 25, but that doesn't apply to foreigners. Nor to me.

Note that 46 Doung 2/9 is a new location of Cloudy, and is not listed online anywhere, but it does in fact exist. It's a big two-story balcony shop space. You can't miss it.

Che Lien

Branch 1: 189 Hoang Dieu (near Food Street)

---

3. https://maps.app.goo.gl/WggqrtLMQkxtrxmt6

Branch 2: 399 Nguyen Tat Thanh (Thanh Khe what's up!)
Branch 3: Lo16 Duong 2/9 (near Nitrogen Ice Cream)
https://maps.app.goo.gl/3d9em7NV2EfD1SqHA

Che Lien is totally famous and classic che — desserts — in Danang. (*Che* means tea in northern Vietnam, but dessert in southern and central Vietnam. Like tea means lunch in some parts of England.) The only slightly disappointing thing is that even though you'd expect them to make your dessert fresh in the kitchen, if you see the employees working in that back area once they're received your order, actually all they do is dump a pre-mixed packet of your chosen dessert into a bowl. It's still delicious though. Trust me.

The desserts here consist of fruit and jelly-like stuff served in a cereal bowl with ice.

Order from the menu on the wall, then go to the back counter to pick up your dessert, served with a separate bowl of ice. Your basic options are "Thai" dessert with or without durian, or "khuc bach" which is a uniquely Vietnamese (maybe?!) dessert of a bunch of stuff mixed together — grass jelly, almonds, panna cotta, oh just try it already. In fact, at these prices (25K a dish), just get both.

There is a sign in Vietnamese sternly warning you not to eat your dessert in the adjoining park. What they mean is don't bring your entire tray and plates and silverware out to that park. (Yes, people do that. It's Vietnam.) You are, of course, free to get your dessert to go and eat it wherever you want, including that park.

53 PHT

https://maps.app.goo.gl/Yfzruhc1gFJMdhyQA[4]

---

4. https://maps.app.goo.gl/Yfzruhc1gFJMdhyQA

The name refers to its address: 53 Pham Hong Thai. This is a traditional dessert shop kind of like Lien, but the specialty here is *me den*, black sesame. Very cute place on a very cute, quiet back street. With the old-school checkerboard floor tiles, it should be great for your Insta. It feels a lot more homey and a lot less commercial than Lien. They now even have an English menu! Just make sure to ask for it (unless you look obviously foreign, I guess), because there's no English on the menu on the wall or sitting out on the tables, but they do have a menu with English printed on it.

Ut Huu Durian

https://maps.app.goo.gl/jgiE1RNJ7WT6gE1J9[5]

Ut Huu is a durian (that fruit that "smells like hell, tastes like heaven") shop next door to Che Lien. You can buy durians whole or cut up. They do allow on-premises consumption (they have a few tiny stools and chairs), or just take your durian to the benches at the park next door. Please note that durian

---

5. https://maps.app.goo.gl/jgiE1RNJ7WT6gE1J9

is not cheap, so please don't think this place is cheating you if they charge you something like 300K for an entire durian. That's how much durian costs. And cheapo durians sold on the roadside have usually been chemically ripened, or were rejected by wholesalers because of insect infestations or some similar reasons. Durians, like parachutes, shouldn't be bought from roadside randos. Ut Huu is a reputable durianmonger. Trust them for your stinky fruit.

Dua Hien

https://maps.app.goo.gl/hxs9hA6GtWA7EWR88[6]

Dua Hien is a shredded coconut focused dessert shop on Huynh Thuc Khang, the food street. Their specialty is coconut desserts. Which are pretty good.

The only thing at Dua Hien is — there is a very unfriendly vibe here. I thought it was only me, but then I checked their reviews, and all the other (Vietnamese) customers also say that the desserts are good but the vibe is unfriendly. I mean, dessert is supposed to be all about smiles, laughter, happy moments, and insulin resistance, right? This place brings the insulin resistance, but not really the other ones. But the desserts are still good. As the reviews say over and over, the attitude is because the owners of the place are northerners, and that's customer service in the north of Vietnam, aka North Vietnam. Checks out. Besides dessert, they also serve banh duc, which is a classic northern snack of soft rice-flour cubes with shredded shrimp and onions on top. And customers' tears.

Get your beer on

Beer is for some reason really big in Danang. While they do try to sell you the beer experience at Ba Na, you don't need to go that far afield, when the beer right in the city is better.

The first two places are on the city side and more Vietnamese oriented (well, Beer Hub is local oriented, and Kulu is Vietnamese tourist oriented). The other two places are foreign tourist (mostly Korean and American) oriented. Brewhaha is still on the city side, while East West is on the beach side.

Beer Hub

https://maps.app.goo.gl/1HZ2Y28VTpjs1zNu8[1]

Beer Hub is the local beer place I most strongly recommend. You get a big mug of high-end craft beer for 30K VND. Yes, that's about $1.25 USD. You're not expected to tip. They have various types of "German" beer named after various German cities — there's no explanation of how the different types are different, but just give it a try. I think last time, I had the Dresden, and it was pretty good. For 30K, you can't really go wrong.

Plus, Beer Hub has both outdoor and indoor sitting areas, and is great for watching the Hai Chau evening goings-on. You can even kind of see the Dragon Bridge fire show from there, although it's on the other side of the bridge, so you're going to need more than just your beer goggles.

Kulu

https://maps.app.goo.gl/6aaSMB19YCTLjzJD7[2]

---

1. https://maps.app.goo.gl/1HZ2Y28VTpjs1zNu8

Kulu is on the city side and specializes in Hanoi-style bia hoi, light draft beer. It's a bit of a tourist trap for Vietnamese tourists: it's in the part of town known for that. Still, it's a good place to experience bia hoi without the rather rough and unsanitary atmosphere of most bia hoi places.

East West

https://maps.app.goo.gl/GhL4UuDcUPi2ECbGA[3]

This is a non-local beer place. It's on the beach side. There are very few Vietnamese customers. It's a branch of the East West beer chain from Saigon. Prices are about five times higher than those at Beer Hub. You'll get international brand name craft brews though, for 150K VND and up. There's a view of the beach. Food and service are horrid, because this is a tourist place. But if you want beer by the beach in an English-speaking, very foreigner-friendly atmosphere, this is your place.

Brewhaha

https://maps.app.goo.gl/4AyriWZTRGJze2Fo7[4]

2. https://maps.app.goo.gl/6aaSMB19YCTLjzJD7

3. https://maps.app.goo.gl/GhL4UuDcUPi2ECbGA

4. https://maps.app.goo.gl/4AyriWZTRGJze2Fo7

Brewhaha is cool because it's foreigner-oriented it's still locally brewed, and more or less locally priced. A glass will only set you back 50K VND -ish, unlike the 100K+ VND at the more high-falutin' foreigner-targeted beer shops.

The hair wash of a lifetime (plus massage)

You might know from my Saigon guidebook: hair washes are a common way to relax in Vietnam. It's especially a great way to cool down in the heat, or clean up between a day at the office and a social event. This is equally true for men and women. (Speaking of men and women: In Saigon, "men's hair wash" places are a front for prostitution, but not so in Danang. In Danang, it's the "men's haircut" places. What am I even teaching you here?!)

Back to hair washes.

Thi La Spa

https://maps.app.goo.gl/mGHcEXtDQUuho7cr5[1]

Thi La charges 170K for a hair wash. But that's not just a hair wash. That includes a facial, a shoulder massage, a blow-drying, and I forgot what else. You'll get tea before and after, possibly some ginger candy, and yogurt (which is a Traditional Chinese Medicine thing you're supposed to consume together with bathing). It is an awesome experience. 30K is just fine as a tip.

You'll leave your shoes in a locker and put on slippers. I suggest you take a whizz (does that word have an h?) in the bathroom behind the curtain before your one-hour wash, because you're going to have masks on your eyes and face for most of that time. Once you get in the room, they'll give you a silk robe sort of thing and you can strip down as much as you feel comfortable — maybe to your underwear or so. Most importantly, take off your top so they can massage your shoulders and don't get shampoo all over your top.

They also offer services such as massage, waxing, and all the other regular spa services. I really can't speak to those, as I've only experienced their hair

---

1. https://maps.app.goo.gl/mGHcEXtDQUuho7cr5

wash, many times. Note that they do provide hair treatments, but they don't actually cut hair.

I suggest making an appointment at Thi La — the manager speaks English, or have your hotel call. They do fill up often. The stretch of street that Thi La is on is actually full of goi dau places. I've tried most of them, and they are all ok, but none of them approach Thi La (although most of them charge the same 170K). The most Thi La -like of the bunch is probably Da Spa at 51 Nguyen Thi Minh Khai, but it is still not as good as Thi la, and just as expensive.

Mat Xa Nguoi Mu (blind people's massage)

By the way, if you want a local massage experience in Danang: there's a place that has massage by blind people. In Vietnam, massage is one of the few jobs available to blind people (yes, even if they have no disability other than visual impairment). This place charges 120K for an hour massage and you're expected to tip at least 80K. (For price comparison, Thi La charges 500K for an hour massage, and you're expected to tip at least 100K. Yes, Thi La does have a much nicer facility.)

https://maps.app.goo.gl/6HStSk2wpEdtbJXo8

Live music

In Vietglish, live music is "acoustic." It has nothing to do with what's known as acoustic music in standard English. The "acoustic" music in Vietnam could be all electronic, as far as the Vietnamese term "acoustic" goes. Anywhere in Vietnam you see the sign "acoustic," pop in for live music in—but don't necessarily expect to find a shaggy dude strumming an acoustic guitar. (Why the misnomer? Because the most famous live music club in Saigon is named Acoustic—and from that, Vietnamese people have used "acoustic" as an all-encompassing term for live music.)

There are three categories of live music places in Danang.

The first is the style that used to dominate South Vietnam until a few decades ago: a *phong tra* (literally, a tearoom, and yes, I know what that means in British slang). There's only one of these left, Paris, and I absolutely love it, because it's uniquely Vietnamese. But it might not be your thing. It's basically 1960s lounge singers belting out old Vietnamese pop hits and French *chanson* classics. It is so wonderfully Vietnamese though that I urge you to try it at least once if you haven't.

The second is the style that dominates now: an atmosphere that's like a club, with a darkened room and flashing lights and everyone dressed up, and usually a Vietnamese boyband belting out covers of other Vietnamese boybands (or K-Pop). I think this is vile, but it, too, is authentically Vietnamese, kind of.

The third is the foreigner-heavy style that dominates on the east side: alternativey, coffeehousey type stuff, with a lot of Ed Sheeran covers, or sometimes harder rock bands. This is fun, but if you are trying to experience something different in Vietnam, maybe this isn't what interests you.

By the way, there used to be two jazz clubs in Danang. Both have closed down. That's why they're no longer in this book. Sad!

Paris

https://maps.app.goo.gl/KfnnM823z541jC4w5[1]

---

1. https://maps.app.goo.gl/KfnnM823z541jC4w5

Paris is awesome because it's uniquely Vietnamese. Show up around 9 PM and you'll get to hear middle-aged Vietnamese lounge singers belt out South Vietnamese ballads (*nhac sen* or *nhac vang* if you know what that is), French chanson, and the occasional Carpenters hit (what?!).

You can fill out a form to request to sing (usually on another day, but maybe if you're on vacation they can accommodate you the same day) — yes, including English or French language songs if you want. I've never seen a non-Vietnamese person in the audience or especially singing there, but I know that crowd, and they would go nuts (in a good way) for a foreigner up on stage. Singing costs 30K, or 100K if you want them to make a video of you. I can't think of a more awesome (or more Vietnamese) Vietnamese vacation souvenir.

On The Radio

76 Thai Phien, Hai Chau
    https://vi-vn.facebook.com/RadioDaNang/

This is the biggest, loudest, and most bar-like of Danang's live music venues. It really looks and feels like a nightclub more than like a music venue. The customers are almost all in their twenties. Everyone is all dressed up and the guys have super upstyled hair and the girls are all wearing super-tight dresses and lots of makeup and perfume and whatever. Not my scene, but you already knew that. The music is Vietnamese boy band covers or other contemporary Vietnamese pop covers. Or sometimes they go edgy and do a Taylor Swift cover! Yeah, like many music venues in Vietnam, this place used to be good and fun and interesting, and then they found out they could make more money if they just find the sweet spot middle of the market and hit it so hard that it rings! So they don't take any risks here, musically or in any other terms. Service is lacking; nobody comes here for the service anyway. One drink minimum, and that drink costs around 200K. There's a lot of smoking but the strong ventilation system makes the smoke smell not too bad.

The 1920s Lounge

53 Tran Quoc Toan
  https://www.facebook.com/the1920slounge/
  It's called the 1920s lounge, but it doesn't have much to do with the 1920s, other than maybe the interior furnishing style. (Don't worry: those chairs aren't actually a hundred years old.)
  When I wrote the previous edition of this book, The 1920s Lounge used to be like Paris, with old-school Vietnamese lounge singers. Then the owners saw the light, financially speaking. Now they're exactly like On The Radio: anodyne VietPop boy bands. They found the middle of the market and are hitting it so hard that it rings.
  This is basically a smaller copy of On The Radio, with more interesting furniture and more cigarette smoke. It's even right down the street, and looks pretty much identical from the outside.

C Bar

100 Le Quang Dao, Ngu Hanh Son
  C Bar is a foreign tourist oriented bar on the beach side, just down the street from the Yarra Suites hotel I recommended in the hotel section. It has live music 9-11 PM, with foreign (Filipino or Eastern European) musicians doing pretty standard US/UK pop or lite jazz. It's not bad. It won't knock

your socks off, but on the beach side of Danang on a weekday night, your expectations can't be too high, and C Bar isn't half bad. My only qualm about recommending this to you is that there's nothing Vietnamese about this; neither the musicians nor the music is Vietnamese, but if that's what you want, it's cool with me.

Bridges! Breathing! Fire! And Spinning!

Danang's bridges are among its main attractions. The most famous bridge, Cau Rong (Dragon Bridge), opened only in 2013. Before that, people had to take a boat, or a faraway bridge, or even a helicopter across the water. That kind of put a damper on the development of the east side of town, and that's why there's still not much there. There is even a very creepy abandoned airport in Son Tra that nobody needed once the bridges opened.

So the bridges are a big deal.

Let's review the bridges, north to south:

Han River Bridge (colloquially, Turning Bridge / Cau Quay)\

https://maps.app.goo.gl/2WjDwYR2Xs7g5SuVA[1]

Han River Bridge, colloquially Cau Quay (turning bridge), is Danang's northernmost major bridge. As you may have figured out, the Turning Bridge is famous for — turning.

Suppose you've had a long night in Danang. Suppose you've had some coffee and maybe even some alcohol. Who knows, maybe even some of that wacky tobacky (which is very illegal in Vietnam, but in practice widely tolerated in southern Vietnam). It's 1 AM and you're staring out at the Han River bridge, contemplating your life, picking lottery numbers, whatever. And then the bridge starts turning. Rotating about the Z axis. Like spinning in slow-motion. You rub your eyes. It doesn't stop. You look around, expecting to see around you an MC Escher hallucination, but you see only late-night Danang. And that bridge keeps spinning.

---

1. https://maps.app.goo.gl/2WjDwYR2Xs7g5SuVA

Cau Quay turns ninety degrees every weekday night, at about 1 AM, to make way for passing ships. It's like a drawbridge, but instead of swinging up vertically, the whole bridge rotates. You're not hallucinating and there wasn't any peyote in that devil's lettuce you bought from some shady dude on the Cambodian border. That's how the bridge works, buckaroo. At about 3 AM (although exact timing depends on how heavy the ship traffic is that night), it returns to its original position. If you're nearby and awake, you can look.

It's a popular nighttime sightseeing thing—because there's not much else to do at night in Danang! Also because the bridge is near Danang University on the city side, and Vietnamese university students aren't any less fond of late nights than American university students. But did you notice how I said *about* when listing the bridge turning times? Like most things in Vietnam, and especially in Danang, those times are very approximate, so you may find yourself waiting a while if the bridge-turning is late that night. I recommend you ask at your hotel or at a cafe or anywhere else when the bridge has been turning recently, because sometimes they do it as early as midnight, sometimes as late as 2 AM.

Dragon Bridge

https://maps.app.goo.gl/Gd9aQZM5gYJGiHNX7[2]

A big weekly event in Danang is the Dragon Bridge breathing fire and steam, at 9 P.M. every Friday, Saturday, and Sunday evening.

---

2. https://maps.app.goo.gl/Gd9aQZM5gYJGiHNX7

It's not such a huge deal and the whole "spectacle" lasts all of ten minutes maybe, but it's still fun to see. The "dragon" breathes fire (first small then big) followed by water and steam. One of the "fun" things is everyone standing below the dragon gets soaked wet during the water part. Beware. And this is Vietnam, so of course there are vendors selling dry clothes.

It's the east side (the non-city side) of the bridge that breathes fire, so you should ideally be on that side to view it, not the more populous city side.

You can simply hang out on the sidewalk below the bridge, alongside lots of other people. You can also see the fire-breathing from the Son Tra night market, although it's a little bit too far for optimal viewing. The optimal viewing place, according to me, is an otherwise unremarkable cafe right at the foot of the bridge, called Moc Garden Coffee.

Moc Garden Coffee doesn't really have an address, other than "An Hai Trung," the small street it's on, in Son Tra (the east side of the bridge). Basically it's just at the foot of the bridge, on the southeast side of the bridge. A coffee will run you 15K-20K VND. It won't be very good coffee, but that's not the point. The viewing position is excellent.

Note that traffic is banned from the the bridge during the fire-breathing, lest you are getting an epic idea for your extremely viral YouTube channel, VietnamMotorcycleStunts.

Tran Thi Ly Bridge (for cars)

Nguyen Van Troi Bridge (for pedestrians)

https://maps.app.goo.gl/Pd7sJyhpM2kMMyBy9[3]

This is the southernmost bridge, and it's got some great views for a walk. Fun fact: it's named after two famous communist terrori— I mean revolutionaries to kind of cover up the fact that it was built by the US military

---

3. https://maps.app.goo.gl/Pd7sJyhpM2kMMyBy9

in 1965. Anyway, no matter who built it, you should walk it! It's a great place to see the Dragon Bridge, and also to watch the Dragon Bridge's fire-walking show. Note that the barriers at the ends of the pedestrian bridge are just to block motor vehicles from entering. You can feel free to step right over those barriers. No Vietnamese prison, I promise.

Eating Street

Huynh Thuc Khang is a crucial street for you to know if you have a stomach. Or a mouth. Or any interest in food. Or any decency or humanity at all.

HTK, near Dragon Bridge in Hai Chau, is the #1, by far, eating destination for Danang locals. Yes, much more so than the night market or the tourist restaurants you've heard of or anywhere else. It's HTK where Danang eats.

There's also sort of an overflow area of HTK, Hong Dieu Street, just around the corner from HTK — it's HTK's minor leagues, where restaurants start up if they are trying to build up momentum to one day move up to the major leagues of HTK. Or, ignominiously, where some HTK restaurants retreat to when their customer flow and reputation no longer can support an HTK location — it's happened.

HTK is an amazing place to eat in Danang. Let me tell you about some of my favorite restaurants there. Note that there are always new places popping up on HTK, and great places that I just didn't have a chance to review. They are all within a very short stretch of HTK, so just go to any of the places I mention and walk around and see what strikes your fancy. There are also cafes around, for your digestion.

All of the below numbers refer to house numbers on Huynh Thuc Khang street in Hai Chau. It's near Dragon Bridge.

158

Com Hen Thanh

This may very well be my favorite restaurant in Danang. Or in the universe. Hen is clams. And com hen is a deceptively simple dish originating from Hue: clam rice. No biggie, right? Except this clam rice is amazing. It's served with some clam soup, and you're supposed to pour a little bit of that soup over the rice, then drink the rest. They also have clam noodles, and for the hardcore clammers like me, *hen xao*, which is just straight-up fried clams, no rice to get in your way. This place is amazing. And most clam rice restaurants are only open in the morning, but this place is open until 9 PM. The menu on the wall has English translations. I find it hilarious that they leave out the English translations for the *mam* dishes: the ones with stinky fermented fish sauce. Those aren't the specialty here anyway, but feel free to be an absolute madwoman and order those, even if there's no translation.

130

Goi Ca Nam O Sinh

This place serves delicious raw fish salad. You can get your fish salad *kho* (dry, rolled in crushed peanuts) or *uot* (wet, in a marinade). Yes, there's English for everything on the menu. Plus the owners' elementary-school-age kid speaks great English. They even serve one of my favorite dishes, *goi hau*, oyster salad. Yum yum. They even have sizzling beef steak (*bo ne*) if someone in your party doesn't eat seafood. Your fresh sashimi will cost you... 100K. Yes, that's four bucks. Just go. There's another goi ca (fish salad) place, Co Hong, at #118. I think #130 tastes better and is friendlier and family-run, but #130 is actually more popular, so you do you.

63

Bun Thit Nuong Kim Anh

This place has amazing bun thit nuong: that's white rice noodles with grilled pork, cucumber and other vegetables, and (in Danang) sweet peanut buttery sauce.

The menu is only in Vietnamese. But there's not much to it. Under Bun Thit Nuong, the XL size dish is 55K and the big dish is 35K. Like at Starbucks, there's no small. They also sell sausage (nem nuong) or grilled beef wrapped in leaves (bo la lot) — I highly recommend the latter — for 8K a piece, and please order more than just one piece, so as to make it worth their while to prepare it. They have sizzling banh xeo for 60K. And the item at the bottom of the menu is if you just want a plate of the meat in bun thit nuong — 110K for a big plate or 90K for a small plate.

Kim Anh is closed on Sundays.

71

Sabaidi

Sabaidi is a Lao restaurant. And despite the sparse and fair-to-middling Google reviews, it is absolutely hopping almost all the time. It might be the most popular place on this street. There's the usual Lao food: sticky rice and grilled meat, especially sausage and grilled pork. You can also get somtam, Lao papaya salad, called *sum* on the menu. Also, *muc* is squid, and *tom* is shrimp.

Yes, the menu is only in Vietnamese, but the owner speaks basic English, or you can use your Google camera.

120

At 120 is a pretty great eel restaurant, Nghia Tam. The most commonly ordered dish is Chao Luon, which is eel porridge. There's also mien luon, eel noodles. And of course luon xao, which is just fried eel. This is some great eel.

115

Hanoi-holic

As you might imagine from the name, this is a bun cha restaurant. Bun cha is — let me check my notes — grilled pork patty, with bits of grilled pork, in grilled pork broth. With some sour sauce and vegetables, and white rice noodles. We Saigonese folks aren't huge fans of bun cha, but the Northerners love it, as do many foreigners. And in all seriousness, the bun cha here is legit.

145

Bun Mam Ba Dong

Bun Mam is southwestern Vietnamese style stinky fermented fish sauce noodles. Delicious, but an acquired taste. Even many (most?) Vietnamese people don't like bun mam.

61

Bun Quay

Bun Quay is a Phu Quoc (island in southwestern Vietnam) dish: simple rice noodles in a fish broth. Here, you can get your bun quay either with cha tom (basically shrimp bologna) or cha ca (basically fish bologna) in it. Either way, it's 40K. That's under $2 USD for a great bowl of seafood soup. Perfect for a chilly, rainy Danang evening. Or any other time too.

116

Chicky Licky

Stop giggling. This is a "Korean style fried chicken" place — you can get fried, heavily battered chicken nuggets served in a bowl. The grease smell will lead you to the location. Ok, I'm not a huge fan of this place, but other people love it.

51

Jim's House hotel

Don't forget Jim's House hotel, right on Eating Street. It's a good place to stay if you're trying to gain weight. I cover it in more detail in the hotels section.

Other eats

On those "you know you're Vietnamese when" lists, one frequently mentioned item is "if you list eating as a hobby, you know you're Vietnamese." I don't think it's only Vietnamese people who love to eat, but there's some truth to that statement.

Danang has some famous foods. Does it ever. Here's where to eat them. Note that in Danang, as in all of Vietnam, a restaurant serves only one or two dishes, so I'll cover dishes and restaurants simultaneously.

Most of these places do have English menus, and some staff who speak a few words of English. But you should be conversant with the basic Vietnamese food words (for example, *ga* is chicken and *bo* is beef) just in case something isn't translated. And there's always your camera translation app.

Home cooking - Com Me Anh

https://maps.app.goo.gl/AsCvkvA7ZSNNxpBo7[1]

Believe it or not, we Vietnamese people don't eat pho and banh mi every day at home. (Although Northerners do actually eat pho a lot every day at home.) In Da Nang, like in Saigon, we eat a lot of stewed, braised, and caramelized dishes served on rice — yes, that is totally the Cantonese in us. And while that kind of home cooking is almost never found in Vietnamese restaurants outside of Vietnam, it's also slightly rare to find in restaurants in Vietnam. It's just the kind of thing you make at home, and don't go out to eat. Like it's somewhat difficult (not impossible) to find a restaurant in the US that serves peanut butter and jelly sandwiches. Com Me Anh — literally, Mom Anh's Food — serves the Vietnamese equivalent of PB&J. And they're totally

---

1. https://maps.app.goo.gl/AsCvkvA7ZSNNxpBo7

English friendly, with an English menu. Expect lots of braised fish dishes on rice, and lots of soups. Please don't try to order pho. They'll just sigh.

Mi Quang - Mi Quang Ba Vi

https://maps.app.goo.gl/RcrpLqc6czLcudSS7[2]

Mi Quang is, as I like to think of it, "noodles with everything."

It's wide yellow egg noodles with pork, shrimp, peanuts, crackers, seaweed, dried meat, quail egg, and whatever else they put in there. It's kind of a magical dish. *Mi* means egg noodles, and *Quang* refers to Quang Nam, the province of which Danang used to be a part. It's Quang Nam egg noodles.

There's really only one place to get your mi quang on in Danang: Mi Quang Ba Vi at 106 Le Dinh Duong in Hai Chau. And it's cheap, about 35,000 VND. Note that for some strange reason, some sources incorrectly list the address as 166 Le Dinh Duong. It's 106 Le Dinh Duong. They're open from (about) 6 A.M. until (about) 10 P.M. Mi Quang is kind of a breakfast food.

And don't go to any of a number of similar-sounding copy restaurants. Actually many restaurants in Danang are called Ba-something. *Ba* just means grandma, so Mi Quang Ba Vi is Grandma Vi's Mi Quang. Other grandmas have copied Grandma Vi. Don't trust those other grandmas.

Frog Noodles (seriously now)

https://maps.app.goo.gl/ZPSnGc2gqYd4rqiL7[3]

---

2. https://maps.app.goo.gl/RcrpLqc6czLcudSS7

3. https://maps.app.goo.gl/ZPSnGc2gqYd4rqiL7

What goes better together than frogs and noodles?

Hello?

Anybody?

Well, ok. Remember mi quang, the dish I lovingly described above? In Central Vietnam, people sometimes make mi quang with frog meat in addition to pork. You can try it at Mi Quang Ech Bep Tran at 441 Ong Inch Khiem. I think frog doesn't taste like much, and eating frogs from a bowl of soup and noodles is a ton of work — but this is definitely a unique dish, and if nothing else you can tell the story and Instagram it and so on. The standard bowl of frog noodles costs about 120K VND. That's the real price. (I saw some reviews claiming they got "cheated" because they were charged this much. No they weren't. Frogs don't come cheap!) The only negative about this place is they charge 20K VND for a bottle of water and don't have free iced tea. That's kind of outrageous in Vietnam, but I trust you won't allow it to spoil your vacation.

Bun Thit Nuong, Bo La Lot, Nem Lui - Ba Trai

https://maps.app.goo.gl/MLpfQoxCn7ubfGH29[4]

Bun thit nuong, bo la lot, and nem lui are three separate dishes, but because they involve a similar method of grilling meat, they are usually served by restaurants that specialize in those three dishes.

---

4. https://maps.app.goo.gl/MLpfQoxCn7ubfGH29

Bun thit nuong is white noodles with grilled pork, vegetables, and a gravy-like or Thai-like thick brown peanut sauce. Saigon also has bun thit nuong, but in Saigon, it's served with (or in) nuoc mam, clear fermented fish sauce, not the peanut sauce used in Danang.

Bo la lot is an "only in Danang" dish. (That's not literally true, but you know what I mean.) It's ultra-thin slices of beef, like shabu-shabu, wrapped in green leaves of the la lot plant, then grilled in those leaves. You eat the whole thing, including the leaf wrapper. The taste is amazing. The outer leaves are a crunchy shell. The marinated beef flavor inside is wonderful. I normally don't eat beef, but I love bo la lot, a lot. (Sorry, but you should've seen that pun coming.)

Nem lui are ground pork patties molded around lemongrass skewers, and served with a brown sauce. The lemongrass skewers give the ground pork a tangy flavor. Nem lui is usually associated with Hue, the "royal" city near Danang. And the nem lui at Ba Trai is the best in Danang. Trust me.

Yes, the constant grilling does take its toll on the building, and it's smoky and maybe not even so perfectly clean inside. The employees don't speak English, but all you need to say is bun thit nuong, bo la lot, and nem lui, which are also the things they expect you to say, so how difficult can it be?

It's a family place. Service is quick and friendly. Prices are low. This is absolutely my favorite restaurant in Danang. Go. Eat. Now.

Bun Cha Ca - Hon

https://maps.app.goo.gl/A6xiibgQn8vDQ3NZA[5]

Bun cha ca is fish-cake white-noodle soup, associated with Vietnam's central coast, especially Quy Nhon and Danang. Fish cake is like fish balls, only flat. Maybe it's a bit like processed meat, but made from fish. Anyway, it's good, and it makes a great soup. For the pho-obsessed foreign tourists: it's like fish pho! It's a hot steaming bowl of noodles and broth. Hon at 113 Nguyen Chi Thanh in Hai Chau is by far the most famous place to get bun cha ca in Danang.

Warning: Hon is inside the alley at 113 Nguyen Chi Thanh. You have to go into the alley, and a few shops down, and Hon will be on your left side. There is a fake (because of course there is) of Hon at 113 Nguyen Chi Thanh on the main road. Make sure you go to the one inside the alley, not the fake one that's on the main road at 113 Nguyen Chi Thanh.

Com Hen - Quan Com Hen

https://maps.app.goo.gl/KMdizCcb8aSaryBw9[6]

Com hen is a breakfast food along Vietnam's central coast. It's rice mixed with chopped baby clams. Instead of rice you can also get white noodles, in which case it's bun hen. You can often find com hen sold on the street in Danang in the early mornings, until around 9 A.M. This restaurant, in Thanh Khe, claims to sell com hen all day, until 10 P.M. Well, you know how that

---

5. https://maps.app.goo.gl/A6xiibgQn8vDQ3NZA

6. https://maps.app.goo.gl/KMdizCcb8aSaryBw9

goes—I still recommend you go there in the morning (they open at 6AM) to make sure you actually get some com hen. Quan Com Hen. 95 Ong Ich Kiem, Thanh Khe, a bit south of most of the stuff in Thanh Khe. Note that there's another highly recommended com hen restaurant on Food Street. I actually slightly prefer Thanh, the com hen restaurant on Food Street, but Quan Com Hen is also excellent, and preferred by some of my friends.

Banh Xeo - Ba Duong

https://maps.app.goo.gl/j6vK9TT58GfDKVKS6[7]

Banh xeo is an onomatopoeic name for a sizzling rice-flour pancake with meat (or tofu) fillings and dipping sauce. Ba Duong, pronounced *ba yoong*, a shop down an alley, has gotten a reputation as Danang's most famous banh xeo—with a uniquely Danang dipping sauce.

Banh xeo actually originates in southwestern Vietnam, the Mekong Delta region known as mien tay between Saigon and Cambodia, but Ba Duong puts a Danang take on banh xeo, making it with a dipping sauce rather than the clear fish sauce with which it's usually served in mien tay and Saigon. Ba Duong is at K280 / 23 Hoang Dieu in Hai Chau. That means it's house number 23 on the alley at K280 on Hoang Dieu. You'll find it. It has crowds. Ba Duong (remember, ba just means grandma, so this is Grandma Duong's banh xeo) also serves bun thit nuong, bo la lot, and nem lui, just as my favorite, Ba Trai does. I think Ba Trai is better for those specialties than Ba Duong. Let Ba Duong stick to her banh xeo and leave the btn, bll, and nl to Ba Trai. But if you want to eat those dishes and are already at Ba Duong, well, go for them, because they're not bad, just not as good as they are at Ba Trai. That banh xeo tho.

---

7. https://maps.app.goo.gl/j6vK9TT58GfDKVKS6

Bun Bo Hue - Ba Dieu

https://maps.app.goo.gl/PQbUiRLcWBMjWVST6[8]

Bun Bo Hue is Hue-style beef noodles. I was once on a domestic flight in the US, and the clever teenage guy sitting next to me, upon finding out I'm from Vietnam, asked me, "In Vietnam, is Vietnamese food just called *food*?" I'm here to tell you that around Hue, Bun Bo Hue is just called bun bo. And the best place for it is called Ba Dieu (pronounced *ba yoo*), at 17 Tran Tong in Thanh Khe, slightly north of the central Hai Chau area in Danang.

The bun bo is just as it should be—a bit smokey and caramely. Note that this place is only open 2 P.M. - 8 P.M. and it looks like it's in the middle of nowhere but it's fine, just next to some empty lots. Relax.

Banh Mi - Banh Mi Ep Huong and Banh Mi Ba Lan

Banh mi in Danang is a bit different from Saigon and Hanoi banh mi. The usual banh mi in Danang is "banh mi que," meaning stick banh mi.

It's thinner and crispier than other Vietnamese banh mi, and it's usually put into a toaster oven for a few seconds before it's handed over to you, to make it warm and crisp. Pretty good, right? You can find banh mi que (stick banh mi) on sale from food carts all around the urban parts in Danang. You'll pay around 3,000 VND for a plain stick of banh mi or around 15,000 for a full banh mi sandwich. But if you want a restaurant wholly devoted to banh mi—and great banh mi at that—there's Ba Lan, Ep Huong, and Cham Pate.

Banh Mi Ba Lan (62 Trung Nu Vuong in Hai Chau) is only open 3PM-11PM, and serves famous smokey banh mi.

https://maps.app.goo.gl/nveJ8Kb1Qgs8eaRQ9

---

8. https://maps.app.goo.gl/PQbUiRLcWBMjWVST6

These are not as big and soft as the huge pillow-soft Saigon banh mi. They're smaller and crispier. And after their turns in the coal oven, they smell a bit like smoke. No, it's probably not good to eat something smoke-flavored every day, but put it in perspective and consider all the cigarette and motorcycle smoke most Vietnamese people breathe.

Banh Mi Ep Huong on the beach side has what Americans call panini: pressed bread sandwiches. "Ep" means pressed.

https://maps.app.goo.gl/WaY2EdREBbWQuVBz6

They start out as regular Danang banh mi, and then Elly sits on them. Ok, not really, but that's the effect. They're pressed. And they're good, although pressing takes out all that pillow-fluffiness from the bread. And since this place is really out in the middle of nowhere on the beach side, most people just order it for delivery on Grab Food. The good news is that they really genuinely are open 24 hours a day (for delivery)! Ask me how I know.

Banh Mi Cham Pate in the alley at 28 Chu Van An in Hai Chau serves banh mi with pate and mystery meat to a crowd of hungry college students every morning—it is crowded, you might see some pushing in line, but they do have English there—theoretically 6 A.M. until 10 A.M., but in practice, don't count on them being open after 9 A.M.

https://maps.app.goo.gl/YLL2ScSc1bHVQ6AC7

They also serve the same pate and processed meat on sticky rice, xoi. So when you go up to order, they will ask you whether you want banh mi or xoi. I recommend banh mi, but if you want to try something new, I suggest you get one banh mi and one xoi. They cost about 30,000 each.

Fusion Tacos - Taco Ngon

https://maps.app.goo.gl/UKSqP7gT51N6U2Nc6[9]

This is a dark horse entry. But it's so much fun. It's on the south part of the beach side (83 Hoang Ke Vien, https://www.facebook.com/tacongon/[10]), away from everything except the expat areas near the beach. And it's a taco stand. The tacos aren't particularly authentic-Mexican, but they're wonderful, and the place is just a lot of fun.

Most of the customers are Americans (although Vietnamese hipsters go there too, cough cough), and the boss is Taiwanese, and the employees are friendly and speak excellent English. They have fish, chicken, and pork tacos, with a variety of sauces and toppings.

The price is 40K VND for each taco, which is pretty expensive for Danang, especially when you probably need two to feel full.

---

9. https://maps.app.goo.gl/UKSqP7gT51N6U2Nc6

10. https://www.facebook.com/tacongon/?locale=vi_VN

Uniquely Vietnamese: Cao Dai temple

Cao Dai is the only exclusively Vietnamese religion. And while tourists generally believe there's "the" Cao Dai temple in Vietnam—the one that tourists go to in Tay Ninh—there are Cao Dai temples all over South Vietnam.

You may have heard of Cao Dai. Novelist Graham Greene famously wrote about it. And Cao Dai is the correct answer to the trivia question "What religion venerates Victor Hugo as a saint?" Yes, Cao Dai venerates Victor Hugo—along with Sun Yat Sen and Nguyen Binh Kiem—as the highest level of saint, because of the belief that in *Les Miserables*, Hugo showed a saintly wisdom about human suffering.

Cao Dai was illegal in Vietnam from 1975 until 1986, and for that reason, Cao Dai is more active in the United States than in Vietnam. Now Cao Dai is legal—although closely watched, because it's closely associated with anti-communism, and it tends to be quite interested in politics and government. The group of Cao Dai adherents that built Danang's Cao Dai temple was formed as a nationalist force to try to prevent Japanese occupation of Vietnam.

Vietnam—or a Vietnamese community in the U.S. or Australia—is the only place where you can see a Cao Dai temple. I think it's worth checking out, because it's one of those "only in Vietnam things," and there's a Cao Dai temple comfortably in the middle of Danang. You're welcome to come in and wander around—just take off your shoes before entering worship areas, and try to put some money in the donation box (10,000 VND is fine). If you want to be really correct about it, men should only use the gate marked "nam" and women should only use the gate marked "nu," but even we Vietnamese people sometimes ignore this bit of protocol, so don't worry about it too much.

I suggest you read up on Cao Dai before you visit the temple, so you have an idea of what you're looking at. I'm not a member of Cao Dai, but I think it's an interesting part of Vietnamese culture. You can see the repeating motif of the eye—that is the left eye of god watching over humanity. "Cao dai" literally means "tall big" in Vietnamese and Cantonese. In any Cao Dai temple, there is a strong theme of climbing upward, higher and higher.

https://maps.app.goo.gl/UdT6cZEKXUUzEdkYA

There is a ceremony at noon, 6 P.M., and midnight every day. Going at the time of the ceremony allows you the chance to see the procession and ceremony, but on the other hand, going during the ceremony prevents you from wandering freely around the temple. And yes, as you've heard me say about other things in Danang—the midnight ceremony sometimes doesn't happen at all, so stick to noon if you really want to see the ceremony.

The Cao Dai temple is at 63 Haiphong in Hai Chau. There's no admission fee, but it's polite to leave a small donation (10,000 or 20,000) in the donation box. No official dress code, but have some common sense about going to a house of worship. Also, no official prohibition on photos, but again, use common sense when people are worshiping inside.

Musea

Danang is only about three hundred years old, so it doesn't have much ancient history, but as it becomes a major Vietnamese city, it's getting museums (I said *musea* above just to be precious, sorry) befitting a major city. One more Vietnamese term you might need: *bao tang* means museum. If someone asks you where you're going, you can tell them you're going to the *bao tang*. There used to be a Danang city museum at 24 Tran Phu, but it closed down at the end of 2024, supposedly "temporarily."

Cham Sculpture Museum

2 Duong 2/9, Hai Chau

Big yellow building at the corner of Bach Dang and Tran Phu, in Hai Chau, near Dragon Bridge

This is the big museum everybody recommends, built by the French colonialists in the early 20th century. Before its being an official museum, in the early 1900s it was an informal collection of Cham sculpture collected (stolen?) by various French collectors and brought to Danang. The Cham people are the Hindus, later Muslims, descended from Malays and Indonesians who previously ruled Vietnam's southeastern coast. The museum of their sculpture interesting, although don't expect too much and certainly don't make a whole-day affair of it. You can have a very good look at the entire museum in less than an hour. Also, there's no air conditioning, so be wary of hot days. 60,000 VND admission. 7 A.M. - 5 P.M.

Da Nang Fine Art Museum

78 Le Duan, Hai Chau

This museum opened in December 2016, and is Da nang's unofficial entry into the big leagues as a city. Previously, only Saigon and Hanoi had fine arts museums. Now Danang gets one too. It has about five hundred items, mostly paintings, and there's a strong emphasis on Soviet-style social realism that you might enjoy in a propaganda-kitsch kind of way. 20,000 VND admission (free for students and people over 60, including foreigners), open 8AM-5PM.

Beaches and surfing

We Vietnamese people only go to the beach in the early morning, around sunrise, to exercise and sometimes for a morning wash-up. We're gone once the sun becomes too strong, and then we come back in the evening to hang out with our friends and maybe take a dip again in the water after sunset.

That means that during the day, the foreigners have the beach all to themselves / yourselves.

If there's any crowding during the day on a Vietnamese beach, it's going to be from foreigners (unless it's Vietnamese instagrammers who just drop by to take pix). And as a corollary of that, local-dominated beaches won't be crowded during the day.

While most of the beaches — especially for foreigners — are on the east side, don't neglect Thanh Khe, north of the central city. It's a great beach as beaches go, even if it's next to a busy road and urban area.

I'll cover the more foreign-popular beaches, especially My Khe, but do me — and more importantly, yourself — a favor and don't forget the often overlooked (by foreigners) beaches just north of the central city.

My Khe beach (east side, south)

https://maps.app.goo.gl/jQ43ik7LyGoNxNex6[1]

My Khe is the most popular beach for foreigners in Danang. It's what was called China Beach back in the day. And sure, there are miles (literally!) of soft sand and breaking waves and so on. But it's been so developed and commercialized, and most anywhere you go, you'll get hit up by grandmas trying to hawk beach chair rentals or beer or whatever.

---

1. https://maps.app.goo.gl/jQ43ik7LyGoNxNex6

The most popular area of My Khe for foreigners is the southern part, near the An Thuong -named streets; that's also where the beach hangout places are. (Check out Burger Bros on An Thuong 4 if you want a burger and likely the company of other beach goers).

If you want to experience the beach Vietnamese style, go around sunrise. But if you, like most foreign tourists, visit the beach during the day, the only Vietnamese people you'll find there will be grandmas who will rent you beach chairs for around 50,000 VND for the day. They may also have towels, sodas, snacks, and whatever else you need. There are usually competing groups of grandmas (and yes, they're always grandmas) roaming the beach offering their chairs and snacks, so if one grandma cartel quotes you an outrageous price, you may want to wait for the next bunch. Note that there aren't convenience stores around the beaches, so either bring your own water and snacks, or wait for the grandmas; of course, BYO will be cheaper. In the evening, especially after sunset, snack vendors do pop up, but they're Vietnamese-speaking and catering for the people hanging out on the street near the beach, and usually don't go onto the beach itself.

If you plan on going in the water, avoid the part of the beach near the bunch of beach-side seafood restaurants. You can guess where the sewage from those restaurants goes. Yes, this is Vietnam.

Generally the water is rough but shallow, so be careful. There are no lifeguards, so again, be careful. If you want to surf, note that there are strong currents, and the wave break area is quite a ways away from shore, so... be careful.

There's an expat-centered surfing community on the streets around An Thuong 1-8 in the southern part of the beach area.

The epicenter of the surfing community is Surf Shack, which is right in that warren of An Thuong streets:

https://maps.app.goo.gl/2n4HVaYGJT2RQfbH9

https://www.surfshackvn.com/

Foreigners tend to assume the Surf Shack folks are Vietnamese, but actually they are Japanese. They charge $60 an hour for a private lesson (including board rental), which is not outrageous — ten years ago, there was a German dude charging $75 hour, and that was ten years ago, and he had lots of customers.

But don't overlook Danang Local Surf School: a smaller, cheaper, and more local option, with Vietnamese (hooray!) instructors. Yes, they speak fluent English and have English-language classes. These are nice folks at DLSS, although not as famous as Surf Shack, so here's a shoutout for them:

https://maps.app.goo.gl/iSjH8ddWob5oQmgt8

Pham Van Dong beach (east side, north)

https://maps.app.goo.gl/RV8J3TTBn8w5qMCs9[2]

PVD is a very local beach in the early mornings and evenings, around sunrise and sunset. Because of the soft sand, lots of people do something like a salt-mud bath, rolling around in the wet sand and then letting themselves dry off like that. Some think it's for beauty, while others do it just for fun. Join them. Note that you can only swim in places where you see a lifeguard (look for

2. https://maps.app.goo.gl/RV8J3TTBn8w5qMCs9

the word *cuu* written in red on a stand); otherwise, stick to splashing around in the waves. During the day, when the foreigners use the beach, lounge chairs are for rent for 40K-50K for the day. Drinks and snacks are available from roaming vendors for similar prices.

Man Thai beach (east side, far north)

https://maps.app.goo.gl/KAMbggELwSac5TbW9[3]

Man Thai is an east-side beach that seldom sees any tourists. It's true that it doesn't have quite the expanses of white sand that My Khe has. But it also doesn't have the tourist crowds. Nor the vendors and lounge chair rentals and the like. It's pretty unspoiled, which (perhaps ironically?) is unusual for a beach-side beach.

Nguyen Tat Thanh (Lien Chieu) beach (city side, north)

https://maps.app.goo.gl/V4m1KFxE91Jh59B36[4]

This is the overlooked, underrated, seldom-foreign-tourist-visited beach just north of Danang's airport, on the city side. It faces north-ish, and tends to be a bit windier, with rougher waters, than the quieter waters of My Khe and the east-side beaches.

---

3. https://maps.app.goo.gl/KAMbggELwSac5TbW9

4. https://maps.app.goo.gl/V4m1KFxE91Jh59B36

Check out Blue Sea Coffee. It's right on the beach (*on* the beach, not across the road!), and it's definitely a vibe. Only opens around sunset. Not open in the mornings.

https://maps.app.goo.gl/pkWTFLP5kMJhDnU76

Serious seafood

Ca An Kien Seafood restaurant (city side)

https://maps.app.goo.gl/VQbxPeJCHpybQfqK6[1]

Right on the city-side beach (or across the road from it at least), with a view of said beach, this is where you get your seafood on.

The main market of this restaurant is big groups going out at night. Hence the large portions (meant to be shared) and the heavy emphasis on selling you booze (you don't have to accept). You'll do fine here as a solo diner in the middle of the day — I'm just telling you that you might find the restaurant empty in the middle of the day, which doesn't mean that local diners are avoiding it.

They specialize in fish dishes, mostly locally caught fish. Unfortunately, I don't know which of the fish is caught locally (and exactly how close to the restaurant the fishing boat would have to be to be considered "local," for all you locavores). But you can ask: "Ca bat o day, khong?" means "Fish caught here, Y/N?" and you can ask that while pointing at a fish dish. *Bat* sounds like the Thai currency *baht* and not like the flying mammal.

There's no English menu. But this isn't hard stuff. The menu is printed on a very clear black-and-white font that will be good for your camera translation. And you also have me. I'll recommend, and translate the names of, some dishes. Let your camera translation or AI assistant do the rest.

The first section I encourage you to consider is *GOI*. Those are seafood salads, basically chopped seafood and fruit and vegetables, eaten as an appetizer.

Goi hai san tai Thai is "Thai style" spicy-sour seafood salad.

Goi hoa chuoi trom tom thit is shrimp and pork with banana flowers

So Mia Bop Chua is clam salad.

---

1. https://maps.app.goo.gl/VQbxPeJCHpybQfqK6

Goi sua is jellyfish salad.

Goi ca trich is the herring salad I always recommend you try at other restaurants

And then I recommend you move on to the page labeled *CAC MON CA*, which means all types of fish.

You choose your fish on the left side, and your preparation method on your right side. There is no price listed on the menu because it's all "market price." I would expect prices for each dish to be in the 200K-400K range, but make sure to ask clearly — you are extremely unlikely to meet an overpricing scam here, but it's possible to have a simple miscommunication.

The first list is labeled "beach fish," which means saltwater fish.

Ca mu is grouper

Ca suu is snapper

Ca hong bien is red snapper

Ca nhong is barracuda

Ca dia is rabbitfish

Ca chai is mackerel

The second list is "sweetwater fish," which means, ok, you know what it means.

Ca chinh suoi and *ca chach que* are both eels

Ca keo is a tiny sardine-like fish, technically a perch (I feel like a marine biologist here)

Ca nau is a catfish

Ca diec is a carp

And then cooking methods:

Nuong muoi ot: Grilled with salt and hot pepper

Nuong moi: Grilled without seasoning

Hap xi dau: Steamed with soy sauce

Hap ngu lieu: Steamed with spices

Nau rau ram: Cooked (maybe pan-fried) with herbs

Sashimi 3 mon: Three-way (I don't know why three) sashimi

Be Man (beach side)

https://maps.app.goo.gl/qw82EkJGdKcHPBWbA[2]

Be Man (pronounced *beh mahn*: it means the baby, usually a colloquialism for a cute young woman, named Man) is the most famous, longstanding seafood restaurant in Danang. Yes, it's very local-focused, but, well, isn't that usually the sign of a good restaurant? They do have something of an English menu — just don't expect perfect English from the menu, nor from the designated English speaking waiter they'll send to your table. I guarantee Be Man will be cheaper, fresher, and a lot more authentic than the more foreigner-friendly seafood places. Can you handle it? I think so.

Cua Dat (beach side)

https://maps.app.goo.gl/pyQwm33Awgp582dTA[3]

Cua Dat is an example of one of those seafood-restaurant rules of Vietnam. Generally the best places are the ones not right near the beach. For obvious reasons. They trade on their food, service, and prices, not on their proximity to the beach. And spending less on real estate lets them spend more on food and service. Cua Dat is great, and is surprisingly English-friendly. They do have English on the menu, and some of the waitstaff do speak passable English. Cua Dat is expensive as far as local seafood restaurants go, but still much cheaper — and a much better value — than the tourist-oriented places.

---

2. https://maps.app.goo.gl/qw82EkJGdKcHPBWbA

3. https://maps.app.goo.gl/pyQwm33Awgp582dTA

Moc (beach side)

https://maps.app.goo.gl/bxbD4m7i7cdhom2M8[4]

Moc is the king (or queen?) of Google reviews of seafood restaurants in Danang. I think it's overrated — they almost bully customers to give reviews — but it's still good. It's a lot foreigner and English friendlier than the above places. Yes, that also means a bit more expensive. I've sent foreign acquaintances unfamiliar with Vietnam/Asia to Moc, and they were very happy — I'm not sure whether they would've been happy at a more "local" place such as Be Man or Cua Dat.

---

4. https://maps.app.goo.gl/bxbD4m7i7cdhom2M8

Marble Mountains

https://maps.app.goo.gl/uq5sUzCsCtvZNS2N6[1]

They're five small mountains on the south side of the beach side of Danang. In English, they're called Marble Mountains, or in Vietnamese, Ngu Hanh Son.

Most hotels sell tours going there, but getting there is just a normal taxi or Grab car ride from Danang (especially from beach-side Danang). A Grab car costs about 100,000 VND from the city side of Danang, or about 50,000 from the beach side.

The Vietnamese name, *Ngu Hanh Son*, means five marble mountains. It's also the name of the surrounding neighborhood.

The five mountains are named after the five elements from Chinese and Vietnamese mythology: water, metal, earth, fire, and wood. The tallest mountain is Thuy, water, and that's the one that has an elevator, and is the only one open to the public.

Also, there are marble sellers all around. The merchandise they're offering comes from factories in China — and there's nothing wrong with knowingly buying that (don't believe their claims that it's local natural marble blah blah), but you can find the same "marble" cheaper on Ebay or Amazon, so why bother buying it here? The real marble sculpture from the marble mountains that you might see local Vietnamese craftsmen hand-sculpting usually goes to well-connected well-off Vietnamese collectors, not to the small-time sellers pestering you to buy something.

As with any tourist attraction in Vietnam, I suggest you go early in the morning on a weekday to get the place to yourself. However, Marble Mountains never gets that crowded outside of Vietnamese holidays. It's not like Ba Na, where you have to work really hard to avoid the crowds. So don't stress

---

1. https://maps.app.goo.gl/uq5sUzCsCtvZNS2N6

yourself if you can't wake up at 7 AM to get here early. Just try not to go on a weekend, and especially not anytime near Tet.

Marble Mountains are on the way to Hoi An, so you could do them as a combined trip if you want, but I really don't think that's worth it. First, Hoi An is an evening place, and second, Marble Mountains are best in the early morning. And second, the amount of Grab Car money you'd save is negligible by combining the trips — Marble Mountains are only about 100K VN from Hai Chau, or 50K outside the beach side — and if I were you, I'd rather rest up and just do one destination at a time.

Entering

There are two possible entrances to Ngu Hanh Son. The first is the more local one, the one without the buses, and the one with a few marble sellers and an entrance ticket booth marked only in Vietnamese.

That first entrance you encounter when coming from Danang is the one I recommend you use. This is the one without the buses and without the elevator. There's a little coffee shop there that I highly recommend as your starting point and staging area. Their coffee is really good! Just watch out for dudes offering to sell you tickets to the mountain or trips to Danang or Hoi An or whatever — mostly scammers, though some are just poor local dudes trying to make an honest buck, offering unofficial tours or whatever. You really don't need a guide. It's all a very well-marked, very obvious tourist attraction.

At this non-bus area, there's a very communist-looking ticket office marked only in Vietnamese. If you want, you can buy your ticket right there. 40K. According to the reviews, they sometimes try to charge more. I haven't tried my "konichiwa, I am from Japan!" bit here, so I don't know how often that happens. (I don't pretend to be Korean because a lot of people in Danang's tourist industry can speak Korean, and I'd be instantly found out.)

Unfortunately, this decidedly sleepy office only sells tickets to the mountain itself, not to the elevator. To buy a ticket for the elevator, you'll have to go to the much more touristy and crowded and hectic entrance nearer the elevator. By the way, I'm not recommending anything, but because this is the local entrance, it's not really policed. You can just walk right past that ticket office and right on up those stairs to climb the mountain and it's unlikely anyone will bother you.

It's quite a steep and exhausting climb up those stairs, taking at least an hour if you're in good condition. I recommend you take the elevator. That elevator costs only 15,000 extra roundtrip — but it does require a lot of waiting in line, first to buy the elevator ticket, then to get on the elevator.

To get to the entrance with the elevator, follow the blue sign and go to your right (as you're facing the stairs).

If you proceed to your right, the first ticket seller booth you'll encounter is the one for the cave. It's an ok cave.

I know I sound blase. Actually the cave would be spectacular if it weren't always full of yelling tour groups (mostly from India). But for 20K, it's worth a peek.

Depending on your physical fitness, there's actually a lot to explore inside that cave. It's all paved and illuminated, but it still takes some physical fitness to go up and down all those networks of steep stairs. And it theoretically opens at 7 AM (I'd say give them until at least 7:30 AM to show up for work) so if you come early, you can beat those crowds and actually get the cave to yourself. Don't miss the illuminated sculpture of a male appendage!

As you continue to the right, you'll finally get to the main ticket booth — the one with the huge line of tourists! It's sort of not the ticket sellers' fault that the line is always long, as it seems every tourist takes a very long time to conduct a very simple transaction.

You'll pay 40K for your mountain ticket, and 15K for your elevator ticket. Make sure to hold on to both tickets, as on the elevator side, they do random "ticket checks" at random points, even on top of the mountain. Since you might have just climbed up the elevator shaft or something.

The elevator ride is pretty cool. It is a glass-walled elevator (the website incorrectly claims it's a glass-floored elevator). But the glass (plastic, actually) is so dirty and scratched up that you can't really do good photography — but you can still get a decent view of the trip up. The kids will still love it!

Mountaintop

When you exit the elevator, you'll see a map. There are actually a few more caves to explore up at that peak. And while you're sort of at the peak, you're not at the *dinh cua dinh* (Vietnamese slang for awesome, literally meaning *peak of the peak*). You need to follow the map on the sign to wind around and do another fifteen minutes or so of stair-climbing if you want the peak of the peak.

As you might have predicted, the farther away you get from the main elevator entrance, the quieter and less crowded it will get. Hooray.

Even if you took the elevator up, you can take the stairs down. In fact, that's what most people do. So few people take the elevator down that you might have it all to yourself. And they do check your elevator ticket before they let you ride it down; just look for the one in your stack of tickets that says *15,000*.

Danang now has tourist traps!

You know Danang has hit the big leagues, now that it has its own tourist traps. It no longer needs to always rely on Hoi An's tourist traps to supply its tourist-trap needs.

The following are places I recommend you know are tourist traps. Of course, you can still visit them — but go in with your eyes open, knowing not to take their promises at face value.

By the way, don't trust Google Reviews in Vietnam. These tourist traps are prime examples of that: they all have tons of glowing five-star reviews, thanks to various shady rigging methods.

In addition to these specifics, avoid any place with prominent signage in Korean and, to a lesser extent, in English. Avoid any buffets. Avoid anything with buses parked in front, or advertised on buses. Avoid anything priced in USD or KRW.

Son Tra Night Market (Cho Dem Son Tra)

I used to like and recommend this night market. No longer. It's a horrible tourist trap now. There is nothing good there. There's not even any variety in the food: it's all "hello you ma'am lobster seafood you!" touts trying to trick you into spending a few million VND on third-rate seafood that smells like... seafood. There are also a few very substandard food stands selling substandard tourist-friendly dishes like pho and banh mi. There are some souvenir trinkets and fake handbags for sale too, at five to ten times the Alibaba prices the merchants paid for them. There are no local customers, and the very few Vietnamese customers you see are generally tourists who don't know any better. I also have a feeling there are pickpockets at work. If anything, you can go to watch some Korean tourists bargaining over multi-million-VND rancid lobster, but I don't know why you'd choose to spend your time that way.

Danang Downtown / SunWorld Asia Park

When someone refers to Danang Downtown, they're not actually talking Danang downtown (which is probably Hai Chau?). They're referring to an amusement park by that name. A defunct, semi-abandoned amusement park. Until mid-2024, at least its ferris wheel was still operating, even if it was charging a rather steep 150K VND for a spin around. As of early 2025, the ferris wheel is illuminated, but no longer turning. Almost all of the other attractions are closed and non-operating.

Entry is free, even though you have to pass through a turnstile (that they kept around from the days when they charged for entry). What's very scammy is at the entrance they try to sell you ticket packs and all-you-can-ride passes — when almost every single ride inside is closed down. (There might be an occasional carousel running or something.) This is run by SunWorld, the same very well-connected company that runs the amusement park at Ba Na Hills.

It's only "open" (I don't even know what that means in this context) 3 PM to 9 PM.

I find it fun to visit (for free) because I like creepy old abandoned amusement parks. But don't bring your kids here. They'll cry.

Helio Center / Helio Night Market

Oh, the poor, ill-fated Helio Center. It just could never get any traction. It tried many angles. (Snarky me says: But just being a good, honest attraction wasn't one of them.) Most recently, it pitched itself as an *educational center*. Like Danang Downtown, it's almost entirely abandoned and empty. I don't know what the real deal is and why they nominally keep the place open — my guess is that there are foreign (meaning China) lenders or investors or advertisers who think it's still operating. Hilariously, the website (helio.vn) still claims their food court has "130 stools." No, but after you eat there, you might. Thanks, I'll be here all night. Tip your waitress. But don't go to Helio Center.

All *com nieu* restaurants

There's nothing inherently wrong with com nieu. It's claypot rice, and done right, it can be super delicious. It's associated with central Vietnam. But for whatever reason, com nieu restaurants have become synonymous with tourist traps for domestic Vietnamese tourists around Danang. They are all set up for buses of Saigonese tourists — you can see buses parked in front of them, and you can almost see the bus drivers and tour guides collecting their fat commissions for bringing their marks to those restaurants. One big chain of com nieu tourist traps in Danang is Nha Do (Red House), but there are lots of others. Many, but not all, are immediately northeast of the airport.

Nha Bep Cho Han, 22 Hung Vuong (next to Han Market, because of course)

Total extreme tourist trap restaurant. Garbage food at insult prices. This branch next to Cho Han is the flagship of "Nha Bep" (means kitchen) branded tourist trap restaurants in Da Nang. If it has gold frontage, a plaque saying "Da Nang local food," a logo that says "Tran," and a sign in Korean, it's 100% a tourist trap — and this place has all those. In general, avoid the "Nha Bep" restaurant chain in Danang, as much as it's recommended by your hotel or tour guide (I wonder why, cough cough).

Bep Hen, 47 Le Hong Phong

This restaurant has a really nice vintage European-style interior, and somehow gets a Michelin star. Which says more about the Michelin rating system (clueless non-Vietnamese-speaking travel writer parachutes into a city with an assignment to find "an excellent restaurant," while supposedly going undetected by the restaurant management) than it does about this restaurant. In general, the word *bep* in the restaurant's name — which means *kitchen* — indicates a tourist trap. No real reason for that. Just a naming convention for tourist traps.

Tam's Pub and Surf Shop, An Thuong 5

The English-language blogs love this place. Here's the pitch: surf shop, old-lady owner with war stories, amazing Western food. Here's my take: It's a tiny, filthy one-room shop on an out-of-the-way street, with more cockroaches than customers. The food isn't anything special, and since they probably only serve a couple of customers a day, you have to wonder about freshness. The old-lady owner, who is supposedly the big draw, wasn't there the two times I've been there, and while yes, she did live through the war, so did tens of millions of other Vietnamese people. (For censorship-free discussion of the war and tons of stories, it's better to walk into any old-Vietnamese-man hangout in San Jose or Garden Grove, California. They'll talk your head off about the war. Trust me. Some of them are my relatives.)

Ba Na: cable cars to pseudo-Europe

Ba Na Hills were, according to some foreign guidebooks, "discovered" by the French. Gee, thanks. We Vietnamese (ok, originally Cham and Chinese) people had no idea we had these here hills when we lived here for thousands of years! Thanks for discovering them for us!

Snark aside, the European-style settlements in the Ba Na Hills were indeed developed by the French. Like Da Lat, Ba Na was a hilltop getaway for the French colonial elite to get away from the heat and crowding and Vietnamese people (oops) of the cities.

Nowadays, Ba Na Hills host Sunworld Ba Na, a sort of Disneyfied pseudo-European Magic Kingdom tourist park. For about a million dong, you get to ride the awesome and amazing cable cars (round trip, obviously) to a rather cheesy (and semi defunct) amusement park. While the sales pitch is mostly about the amusement park — because they want you to spend time and money there, including staying in their in-house hotels and eating at their in-house restaurants — I think all the value is in the cable car rides. Especially if, unlike their Vietnamese target market, you don't consider "Western" or "European" things to be exotic.

The most important tip for Ba Na

Please, for the love of cafe sua da, go to Ba Na either before or after the tourist crowds. The tourist buses all arrive around 8:30 AM and leave around 3:30 PM. Do like me and get there around 7:30 AM, when they officially open — although usually the employees haven't actually started working yet at 7:30, and you'll have to wait until around 7:50 to get on a cable car. Otherwise, every single thing at Ba Na will look like the photo below — which, mind you, was taken on a Tuesday morning, in the off season.

If you want to avoid crowds but are not an early riser, Ba Na does offer a "Ba Na by night" discount, targeted for Vietnamese tourists, specifically for the evening, after the tourists have left. Unfortunately, the discount is really only 100K VND. The price is 850K instead of 950K. And it includes their dinner buffet, which they claim is worth 600K, but I would not eat for free — it's gross, and unsanitary.

https://banahills.sunworld.vn/en/news-da-nang/ba-na-by-night-a-fairytale-escape-with-a-twist.html

There's something to be said for the sunset views, although I don't think it's so great in the evening — especially since it tends to be cold and foggy. On the other hand, the ticket does apparently include a free drag queen show. I'm not making this up. (Try that in China!)

Tickets to Ba Na

As of 2025, Ba Na tickets cost 950K VND for non-Danang locals. That includes the round-trip cable car ride between the parking lot and the main station, and cable cars within the amusement park. (Many foreign sources seem unaware of the other cable car routes that exist within the park; they're not as long as the main route from the parking lot, but they're fun too.)

There's a discount for Danang locals: they pay 600K instead of 950K. That is actually meant less for giving locals a cheaper way to visit the park, and more for creating a thriving ticket resale industry. Those local discounts are why all the roads to Ba Na are crowded with aunties selling cigarettes and Ba Na tickets — they buy them at the local discount, then resell them to you at the regular non-local price. Of course, if you have a local Danang friend, you can ask them to buy you the tickets at the local price. I'm pretty sure tickets are tickets and nobody will be checking.

https://banahills.sunworld.vn/en/news-da-nang/announcement-ticket-services-prices-list-at-sun-world-ba-na-hills-in-2025.html

LOẠI VÉ / PRODUCT				GIÁ CÔNG BỐ/ PUBLIC PRICE
VÉ CÁP TREO *Cable Car Ticket*	Khách Đà Nẵng *Da Nang Tourists*	Người lớn Adult		600,000
		Trẻ em/Cao tuổi (Trên 70t) Child/Elder (over 70 yrs)		500,000
	Khách Ngoại Tỉnh *Domestics and International tourists*	Người lớn Adult		950,000
		Trẻ em/Cao tuổi (Trên 70t) Child/Elder (over 70 yrs)		750,000
COMBO CÁP + BUFFET TRƯA *Combo Cable Car + Lunch Buffet*				
COMBO CÁP + BUFFET TRƯA *Combo Cable Car + Lunch Buffet*	Khách Đà Nẵng *Da Nang Tourists*	Người lớn Adult		950,000
		Trẻ em/Cao tuổi (Trên 70t) Child/Elder (over 70 yrs)		700,000
	Khách Ngoại Tỉnh *Domestics and International tourists*	Người lớn Adult		1,250,000
		Trẻ em/Cao tuổi (Trên 70t) Child/Elder (over 70 yrs)		950,000
COMBO ĐÊM (lên cáp sau 15h) *Night Combo (Cable Car + Buffet)* - Operating time: from 15h00 - 22h00 - Time for Buffet: from 17h30 to 21h00				
COMBO ĐÊM LÊN CÁP SAU 15H Night Combo - Cable car afTrẻ eme 3PM	Khách Ngoại Tỉnh *Domestics and International tourists*	Người lớn Adult		1,000,000
		Trẻ em Child		800,000
COMBO ĐÊM LÊN CÁP SAU 18H Night Combo - Cable car afTrẻ eme 6PM		Người lớn* Adult		700,000
COMBO ĐÊM LÊN CÁP SAU 19H Night Combo - Cable car afTrẻ eme 7PM		Người lớn* Adult		500,000

Public bus to Ba Na

There is now a little-known (even my Vietnamese friends swear it doesn't exist) public bus from Danang Airport to Ba Na. It is an orange Futa bus, just like the ones that go to Hoi An, and it is route #03. It costs 30K VND each way. It's easiest to catch it from the domestic terminal of the Danang Airport, but you can also catch it from any of the stops in the graphic below. Plug the bus stop location description in the graphic into Google Maps or Grab, or ask your hotel to help you figure it out (though they might claim this bus is "no longer running" because they want you to pay ten times as much for their shuttle).

The best thing about these buses is they run about every half hour, giving you a lot more flexibility than the private buses than run only twice a day — and let you arrive in Ba na before the bus-borne tourist crowds.

https://danangfantasticity.com/en/news/the-bus-route-from-da-nang-airport-to-sun-world-ba-na-hills-is-now-open

https://danang.gov.vn/vi/xe-buyt/danh-muc/chi-tiet?id=39830&_c=139

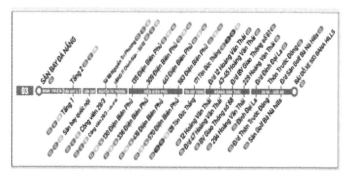

Private shuttle bus

There are private shuttle buses between Danang and Ba Na, for about 150K VND roundtrip. There's a well-known one on Klook:

The big advantage the private shuttles have over the public bus is that the private shuttles will (theoretically; don't absolutely count on it) pick you up at your hotel. Besides being much more expensive than the public bus, the big problem with the private shuttles is they give you a very limited schedule, usually with just one trip per day in each direction. It forces you to arrive at Ba Na exactly when everyone else arrives, and leave exactly when everyone else leaves. That's a guaranteed way to minimize your enjoyment and maximize your frustration.

Grab, or a guy

After the 30% discount for tourist locations you'll get with most any Grab subscription, the one-way Grab fare to Ba Na is in the 200-250K range. That's under ten bucks. I think it's well worth avoiding the indignities of tour groups and buses.

Of course, I also think you should hit up my guy, Mr. Phong (or Mr. Tuan) and see if they can do something better for you than Grab. Maybe it's worth it for you if they're able to keep your stuff in their car while you explore Ba Na, or whatever else. Or maybe you're just more comfortable riding in a nice clean car with an English-speaking engineer (as I mentioned, both Phong and Tuan are engineers by education) than with some Grab rando.

Arriving at Ba Na

When you get there, you'll be dropped off at a big pavilion sort of area. And you can't proceed to the cable cars yet, unless you already have a ticket. (By the way, once you're done, if you're getting picked up, you're only allowed to get picked up at that lobby area if you go to the place that says "Mercure Hotel" — otherwise, you're supposed to get picked up only in the parking lot a few steps away. The rule is enforced variably.)

If you still need to buy a ticket, turn left, and go to the left side of that pavilion. You'll go into a very sketchy looking office that says something like "travel agencies" and be sent to a desk that sells you a ticket for 950K. These are legit tickets, although I think the people at these desks are just randos who bought tickets at the local discount and are now reselling them to you (and obviously, are paying someone to "rent" one of these desks).

Whatever. They do accept credit cards, but there's a 3% surcharge, which you can later dispute with your credit card company if you'd like, as those surcharges aren't allowed — though 3% is only about $1 USD per ticket.

They will try to upsell you to a buffet. That buffet is terrible. I wouldn't eat it for free. Do not accept the buffet upsell. They might try to discount the buffet upsell. Still don't accept it.

By the way, there are tons of food vendors around Ba Na, so don't buy their line that you'll go hungry if you don't get their prepaid buffet.

With ticket in hand, you'll next proceed to the cable car. Look for the signs that say *cap treo* or *ga cap treo*.

What follows is sort of comedic. If you have a good sense of humor.

You will have the longest imaginable walk to that actual cable car station, through a comically unending procession of gift shops, food vendors, photo machines, upsell attempts, and every imaginable grab at your money.

It will seriously take you a good half hour to walk from this entrance to the actual cable car station, going through many hallways, elevators, gift shops, and so on and so on. That's if you arrive before the crowds come. If you come on a bus, together with the crowds, it could take you a few hours to get through the lines and lines and lines.

I think this design is as a way to contain the crowds here as the place fills up — so it never looks like there's a huge line, even if there is a huge line. But if you arrive at 7:30 AM like I do, you will just have a half-hour walk through a lot of escalators, gift shops, and upsell attempts, before you get to the actual cable car station.

On to the cable cars!

Once they've collected your cable car ticket, they tell you that you will no longer need that ticket. You are cleared to ride all the cable cars once you're inside the park.

Try to get your party its own cable car. It shouldn't be a problem if it's not too crowded.

Those cable cars are pretty nice actually. They have some hilarious fake birdsong music playing, and some very tacky voice-recorded ads ("Ladies and gentlemen and boys and girls!" it begins in English), and billboards inside the cable cars, but other than that, they're good. Austrian-made, supposedly. It's usually very hot and stuffy inside the cable cars. The side window should slide open, although I've never been able to get it to do so (maybe only from the outside). But the horizontal windows toward the top definitely do pop open.

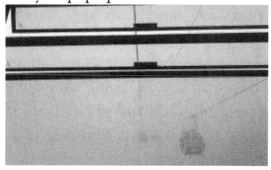

Do like Elly and pop them open for fresh air!

This is the main cable car ride, and takes about twenty minutes. It's a lot of fun. Please don't spend all that time Instagramming and take some time to be present and enjoy the view and the fresh air! Seriously now!

Once you arrive at the station, there are a few other cable car lines going throughout Ba Na. One of the more popular ones takes you to the "golden hands bridge." That's the bridge where — let me check my notes here — golden hands grip a mountain bridge while Chinese pop songs play. Ok, no symbolism or anything, I swear. Anyway, there's a cable car line to take you to that bridge, but you can also easily walk it — as is true for all the cable car lines besides that main first one. There's no way to walk the distance covered by that main first line, but the other ones can be duplicated by walking.

Note that they loudly advertise a funicular ride up and down the mountain. There is no actual funicular ride. It's only planned for some indeterminate time in the future. I did see a construction crew at the site of the advertised funicular so who knows, maybe by 2050?

Snarkety snark snark!

Other stuff at Ba Na

There is a "German" beer hall at "French" Ba Na. The signs in English say that you can get a free glass of beer, but when I asked, in Vietnamese, they just pointed me to the set menus that include a free glass of beer included with a 500K+ VND meal.

There is an alpine coaster that costs 70K VND extra. (If you read my Da Lat book, you know how I love the alpine coaster in Da Lat.) Whenever I've tried to go on the alpine coaster at Ba Na, it's been "closed for maintenance." My guess is they lowkey close it during low season. It looks fun, but don't expect it to be open.

There are bumper cars and other amusement park-ish attractions. When I peeked in on the bumper cars, I saw the most Vietnamese thing ever: the employees fast asleep, using the bumper cars as sleeping pods. Theoretically those bumper cars and other rides are supposed to be included for free with your ticket — and there are some (mostly broken) video games and the like, mostly intended for rainy days.

Cafes because this is Vietnam

Whoever planned Ba Na must not have known that Europeans drink coffee too. There's a remarkable lack of coffee places. Or maybe it's just because they can make more money selling other things. Ba Na has a wildly expensive and unremarkable Starbucks, but I have a different recommendation: a slightly hidden away coffee shop called Rosa Sky.

Go in where you see this sign, near the Starbucks, but on the other side of the building. And take the elevator to the fifth floor.

The interior of Rosa Sky is delightfully faux-French. Get your ~100K drink and sit for hours. You are likely to be the only customer. The employees are likely to be horseplaying, sleeping, or scrolling Facebook, or all three at once. Most of the drinks on offer will be out of stock, and the fruit drinks don't taste like fruit. But you're not there for the drinks. You're there for the view, the atmosphere, and the free wifi. And the charging outlets. Important.

Overnight at Ba Na?

Is overnight at Ba Na worth it? Opinions differ wildly.

There's only one hotel at Ba Na: the Mercure. It costs around 3,000,000 VND per night, or about $120 USD. That's really expensive for Danang, but not so expensive for most places in the world. (The Agoda link at this QR code does *not* have any affiliate commissions. I don't do affiliate programs. I answer only to my readership. And my cat.)

When you walk around Ba Na, you will see "hotels" like the Strasbourg, the Lyon, the Paris, and so on — those are all just different wings of the same Mercure hotel.

For me, spending overnight at Ba Na would feel a bit too Robinson Crusoe. Boring and a bit scary. But other people love it, because you get to roam around the park all by yourself at night. The cable cars aren't running, and there's no place to buy any food or anything, so don't expect too much, but you can indeed wander all the places, including the golden-fingers-bridge (what did I just write?) with almost nobody else around. As you might imagine, that hotel is pretty empty pretty much all year except for Tet.

Getting from Danang to Hoi An

Danang to Hoi An is 30 kilometers (18 miles), so it's not a distant voyage, but it's not just a trivial taxi ride either.

Public bus

The famous Route 1 public bus that used to take you between Danang and Hoi An for 20K VND (and I recommended in previous editions of this book) has been taken out of service. Because crony capitali— um, because reasons.

But there's an alternative: the new Bus 02, just started in late 2024, which is technically two bus trips: Route 02 goes from the Da Nang central bus station (Ben Xe Trung Tam Da Nang) to Vietnam-Korea University (Dai Hoc Viet Han), and Route 02-LK goes from Vietnam-Korea University to Hoi An. If you're taking this between Da Nang and Hoi An, you don't need to get off the bus at the university. Just stay on the same bus. It's the same physical bus, even though it's technically two bus routes. The entire trip takes about an hour one-way from central Danang to Hoi An.

The semi-private bus company Phuong Trang / Futa runs it, using their usual orange vans. You might see their vans running around Danang. They flash the route number; look for the ones that say 02.

Here's the Vietnamese-language announcement of the new public bus route:

And here's the Danang city government announcement about the segment that runs to Korea University:

The initial Danang pickup spot is at the Futa (that's the bus company — and yes, I know what *futa* means in anime slang) terminal at the Danang central bus station, Ben Xe Trung Tam Danang: *ben xe* means bus station and *trung tam* means central.

The Futa terminal is not quite in the same place as the rest of the public bus station. Make sure you're at the Futa terminal, with the orange vans all around. The "bus" is one of those orange vans.

Don't believe guys standing around the bus station, sometimes wearing Grab or Futa jackets, claiming they sell tickets or that the bus is out of service and you should go with them.

Also note that getting to the main bus station from your hotel might cost you around 100K one way, making the trip not much cheaper than Grab Car, so you may want to use one of the other pickup spots around Danang.

The other Danang pickup spots for Bus 02 if you're bound for Hoi An: 59 Ly Thai Tong, 225 Nguyen Tat Thanh, 61 Nguyen Tat Tanh, Grand Tourane Hotel, and Pullman Danang Beach Resort.

Watch for the van-like orange bus and when it's coming, jump up and down and make sure it stops. Many drivers like to pretend not to see waiting passengers. A few of the stops have blue-and-white Bus Stop signs, but most don't. Google Maps generally knows where the bus stops are; trust the location Google Maps gives you, even if there's no sign there.

The buses are supposed to run every 23 minutes, but this is Vietnam, so give it up to an hour. Google Maps claims to know when the buses are scheduled at each stop, but in reality, the bus shows up at pretty random times, and you can definitely wait much longer than 23 minutes. Google Maps is useful for finding the bus stop locations though. It knows those pretty well.

I've attempted to take Bus 02 from Danang (the stop I usually use is 225 Nguyen Tat Thanh) to Hoi An twice. The first time, I waited for forty minutes for it to show up, and it did finally show up. I was the only person all the way to Hoi An. (Protip: Sit up front next to the driver! Nicer seat, seat belt, better view, risk of weird questions if you're a woman.) The second time I tried to take the bus, after an hour of waiting at 225 Nguyen Tat Thanh with no bus in sight, the other two people at the bus stop and I decided to share the cost of getting a Grab Car to Hoi An, because that bus obviously wasn't coming.

The bus stop at 225 Nguyen Tat Thanh is nice because it actually has a blue-and-white "bus stop" sign. Most of the other stops aren't marked at all. (Note however that this bus stop sign claims that the only route that stops there is route 11. That's wrong.)

There's a very bad tourist trap (for Vietnamese tourists arriving in Danang on buses) restaurant next to that 225 Nguyen Tat Thanh bus stop called Pho Bien. Avoid that restaurant. There's also a decently ok ice cream shop called Kem Thanh Binh. The only reason to avoid Kem Thanh Binh is your sugar levels. It's pretty good.

If you don't see a bus after an hour of waiting, it's most likely out of service for the day. No, there's no way to find out in advance, even if you spoke

Vietnamese and called the company. You've just downloaded Life In Vietnam Simulator!

If the bus does pick you up, just tell the driver "Hoi An," and they'll usually sell you a ticket for 35K, or it might be a ticket for 20K at first to the university, and then have you buy another 15K ticket if there's a change of drivers at the Vietnam Korea University stop. That first 20K fare might be lower if you get on farther along on the route. Try to use exact change, or at least nothing bigger than a 100K bill. Their handheld ticket dispensing device is supposed to accept credit cards, though I've never tried paying with a card, and my guess is the drivers will have no idea how to use that functionality.

The Hoi An dropoff spot is in front of the electrical trades vocational college on Nguyen Tat Thanh street. This is what I've verified myself, though it's not what the official listing says it should be. (Just around the corner though, so not a big deal when you're just looking to be dropped off.)

From there, you can walk about fifteen minutes to old town Hoi An, or take a Grab to old town for about 25K VND. Note that this is not where the bus to Hoi An is officially supposed to stop according to its official announcements, but it's where it actually stops, in mine and my friends' experience.

For getting back to Da Nang, the place where the bus will pick you up in Hoi An is not the same place it dropped you off. And also not where the official announcements say it will pick you up. Again, Life In Vietnam Simulator. The bus stop (which is marked with a bus stop sign) for going back from Hoi An to Da Nang is here:

The official name of the pickup bus stop in Hoi An is Cong Ty Det May Hoa Tho, which is the garment factory nearby.

The total cost in each direction is again 35K VND, which is again actually one 20K ticket plus one 15K ticket (remember, two routes technically, though you stay on the same bus). Tickets are sold only on the bus. They may sell you both tickets at once, for 35K total, or one at a time.

Hre are the official announcements, which you can also see on Facebook by scanning this QR (yes, because of how difficult our government makes it for anyone non-connected to get a website, most businesses just use Facebook for their official communications):

TUYẾN XE BUÝT SỐ 02
BX TRUNG TÂM ⇌ ĐẠI HỌC VIỆT HÀN

📍 Lộ trình:

LƯỢT ĐI: BẾN XE TRUNG TÂM - NAM TRÂN - LÝ THÁI TÔNG - NGUYỄN TẤT THÀNH - CẦU THUẬN PHƯỚC - LÊ ĐỨC THỌ - HOÀNG SA - VÕ NGUYÊN GIÁP - TRƯỜNG SA - NAM KỲ KHỞI NGHĨA - TRẦN ĐẠI NGHĨA - TRẠM XE BUÝT ĐẠI HỌC VIỆT HÀN.

LƯỢT VỀ: TRẠM XE BUÝT ĐẠI HỌC VIỆT HÀN - TRẦN ĐẠI NGHĨA - NAM KỲ KHỞI NGHĨA - TRƯỜNG SA - VÕ NGUYÊN GIÁP - HOÀNG SA - LÊ ĐỨC THỌ - CẦU THUẬN PHƯỚC - NGUYỄN TẤT THÀNH - LÝ THÁI TÔNG - NAM TRÂN - BẾN XE TRUNG TÂM.

⏱ Thời gian chạy:

BẾN XE TRUNG TÂM (từ 05h00 đến 18h00) ⟷ ĐẠI HỌC VIỆT HÀN (từ 05h45 đến 18h45)

TUYẾN XE BUÝT SỐ LK-02
ĐẠI HỌC VIỆT HÀN ⇌ CỬA ĐẠI (HỘI AN)

📍 Lộ trình:

LƯỢT ĐI: TRẠM XE BUÝT ĐẠI HỌC VIỆT HÀN - ĐƯỜNG ĐT607 - NGUYỄN TẤT THÀNH - BẾN XE BUÝT HỘI AN - LÝ THƯỜNG KIỆT - TRẦN NHÂN TÔNG - CỬA ĐẠI - ÂU CƠ - BÃI ĐỖ XE BẾN THỦY HỘI AN CỬA ĐẠI.

LƯỢT VỀ: BÃI ĐỖ XE BẾN THỦY NỘI ĐỊA CỬA ĐẠI - ÂU CƠ - CỬA ĐẠI - TRẦN NHÂN TÔNG - LÝ THƯỜNG KIỆT - NGUYỄN TẤT THÀNH - BẾN XE BUÝT HỘI AN - ĐƯỜNG ĐT 607 - TRẠM XE BUÝT ĐẠI HỌC VIỆT HÀN.

⏱ Thời gian chạy:

ĐẠI HỌC VIỆT HÀN (từ 06h05 đến 18h05) ⟷ CỬA ĐẠI (HỘI AN) (từ 05h00 đến 18h00)

The first downside of those public buses is they stop running at 6 PM. Do like we Vietnamese people do and take a bus there, then a Grab car back.

The other downside is that the buses were bought in 2024 by the Vietnamese government from its BFF the terrorist regime in Russia, to help Russia avoid US sanctions 'n stuff. Sorry, innocent victims of Russian terrorism in Ukraine. Anyway, back to talking about getting to Hoi An!

Car

You can take a car to and from Hoi An. It's comfy, and it takes about an hour, depending on traffic and so on.

Grab to Hoi An

Grab Car costs about 300,000 VND one-way, depending on exactly where in Danang you're starting out. Just enter your pick up and dropoff destinations ("Hoi An Old Town" is an available destination) as you normally would in the Grab app and you'll see the fare quoted.

Actually, you might see a bunch of fares quoted. The regular by-distance Grab fare, which is around 450K, then the special Hoi An discount fare, around 360K. Depending on what kinds of discount codes you have and what the surges are like, either one of those might be your best option — usually you can't use discount codes on the already discounted Hoi An fare, but sometimes an undiscounted fare plus a discount code will be cheaper than the discounted Hoi An fare. Got it?

Vietnamese people consider this option expensive, but it's under $15 USD for a long trip between cities in a private car. You might have paid more than $15 for a taxi to the airport back in your home country when you left for Vietnam. This is the comfortable and kind of no-brainer option, especially if you're a few people together and can divide the cost.

For the sake of completeness: yes, Grab Bike is available, and costs around 150K VND between Da Nang and Hoi An. I consider it a death wish — and dirty and uncomfortable — but you do you.

Street rando car to Hoi An

Around Hoi An, any random dude with a car will offer to drive you to Da Nang for 250K, sometimes 270K if he has to give 20K commission to whoever recommended him to you. Those guys also have printed ads posted all around Hoi An. Just know that the going rate is always 250K. The same general 250K fare goes for random guys in Da Nang who want to go to Hoi An, but that's rarer, because generally drivers want to be in Da Nang, not Hoi An.

There will be dudes approaching you in English around the outskirts of Hoi An offering you a ride to Da Nang for 400K, usually waving their phone with the Grab app and saying they are Grab drivers. You know the drill. Those dudes will usually take an offer of 250K, but I'd rather not deal with such scammy drivers in the first place.

I still prefer Grab Car over random dudes, especially if you are a foreign tourist, because getting in some random guy's car is just too risky. It's not even a matter of any nefarious plans or waking up without your kidneys; I'm thinking of random bad events like the car breaking down just outside of town, or the driver being blatantly incompetent or drunk, and a million other things. Obviously, if you know a trustworthy dude (such as Mr. Phong or Mr. Tuan, recommended above) then sure, save the money over Grab Car.

Guys and other car services to Hoi An

You can hit up my guy, Phong, on WhatsApp at +84 98 246 84 61 (or Tuan at +84 90 812 24 67), and I'm guessing he'd take you roundtrip between Danang and Hoi An for around 500K, including waiting for you in Hoi An. That price is just my gut feeling prediction, so ask him directly.

There are a few other car services that promise they'll take you between Danang and Hoi An cheaper than Grab. I can't vouch for them.

My general experience with such services is they may or may not show up, depending on whether they have a better-paying job somewhere, and they may or may not abide by the agreed-upon price. Also, the people at the phone hotline will never speak English, so have your hotel call and arrange:

This service claims 230K rides between Danang and Hoi An:
https://xedananghoiangiare.com/

And this one says 200K on the front page, but then 250K when you go to actually make the booking — yes, this is the kind of stuff you'll have to deal with trying to arrange a ride in Vietnam:

https://xedananghoian.com/

Private shuttle buses

As with many things in life, the most heavily advertised option — private shuttle buses — is the worst one. They cost 150K-250K and are more crowded, less frequent, and have fewer pickup spots than the regular 35K public bus. And if you have more than one person, they're more expensive than a Grab Car.

The fact that all the private shuttle bus companies have websites only in English and quote prices only in USD should already tell you something. We Vietnamese people love to go to Hoi An: why don't they advertise to us? Because we (mostly, usually) know better than to pay 150K-250K for something that's worse than the 35K option.

Actually, the private shuttle buses did have a good market niche some ten years ago, because back then, the public buses to Hoi An were downright scary. Some of the buses on the 01 route didn't even have seats. Those days are gone. The public buses nowadays are a lot like Vietnam Airlines: not great, but less bad than the alternatives.

Note that some bigger hotels may offer you a shuttle to and from Hoi An. It might be worth investigating — though my snarky side says if your hotel offers a bus to Hoi An, you're overpaying for either the room or the bus.

Hoi An overview

If you've been anywhere near any guidebooks or travel blogs, you know the image of Hoi An: yellow sandstone shop houses, and lanterns lighting the canals in the evenings. Hoi An was the commercial center of the ancient Cham kingdom that once ruled what is now Vietnam, and the remnants of Cham and mostly Chinese and French traders now produce a "quaint" tourist attraction in Hoi An's ancient town.

The Cham people—you should read up on them on your own—were primarily Hindus, later converting to Islam, and were descended from Indonesian sea voyagers. Culturally they shared little with the Vietnamese and Chinese, and later the Cham were more-or-less run out of town by the Vietnamese and Chinese. The Cham people do still exist in Vietnam, mostly in Saigon and Phan Thiet, and they are mostly excluded (not by their own choice) from mainstream Vietnamese society, usually working as fishermen, or fish processors, or providing services to other Cham people.

Hoi An, concurrently with being the commercial center of Cham culture, also became the main trading port and commercial center for Chinese (mostly Fujianese) traders in Vietnam. But the most unique thing that happened to Hoi An was not its rise, but its fall. It became a nearly abandoned ghost town in the late 19th century, as the Vietnamese (Dai Viet) and French took over from the Cham and Chinese, and as the Tay Son Rebellion closed most of Vietnam's foreign trade. Whereas most old cities were constantly torn down and rebuilt, Hoi An was abandoned, a ghost town sitting like a preserved specimen, with most of its 19th-century fixtures still intact. While you may encounter some fairy tales about this being due to the Hoi An people's respect for historical tradition, it was in reality due to everyone leaving behind the decrepit ghost town that Hoi An had become in the late 1800s, and nobody caring to tear down or renovate anything old in Hoi An.

Hoi An is an important cultural remnant of the Cham and Chinese cultures, but it really doesn't have much history of Vietnamese culture per se—unless you think of Cham and Chinese culture as predecessors of Vietnamese culture, or unless you consider the modern tourist trade to be Vietnamese culture.

I hate to be blunt, but I'll be blunt: if you hate seeing tourists, don't come to Hoi An. It's a tourist town.

There's nothing in Hoi An these days other than the tourist industry, and almost everyone there is either a tourist or an expat, or someone serving tourists and expats. That's not necessarily bad. But you should know what you are signing up for. Some twenty-year-old guidebooks describe Hoi An as a pristine place not yet discovered by tourists, and that was true when the book was written, but stopped being true about ten years ago.

If you don't mind being around tourists, Hoi An can be a lot of fun. The old town is full of canals and historic buildings—and while the historic buildings have been largely repurposed for the tourist trade, they are still the original structures, even if not used for their original purposes.

Western tourists tend to stay in Hoi An and make day trips to Danang. Vietnamese people and Asian tourists tend to stay in Danang and make day trips to Hoi An. I'm going to make the case for doing things the Vietnamese way, and treating Hoi An as a day trip destination from Da Nang, as opposed to the other way around.

First, your hotel dollar (or dong or Euro or whatever) goes much farther in Danang than in Hoi An. Hotel rooms in Danang are much cheaper than in Hoi An. Not only that, but the hotels in Danang are generally better—more comfortable, more service-oriented, more aware of the need for repeat business rather than trying to fleece one-time backpackers.

Second, Hoi An, despite being touted as a historical or cultural place, really doesn't show you anything about Vietnam. It's like staying inside an amusement park. Not only are the buildings and relics Champa and Chinese, but, as I previously mentioned, Hoi An's whole raison d'etre these days is tourism.

If you don't care to see anything of authentic Vietnam—and I say that in all earnest, without a sneer, because there's nothing wrong with not wanting to see authentic Vietnam—then you should stay in Hoi An. Everyone speaks English and everything is a tourist amusement park. Hey, my parents once went on vacation to Cambodia and specifically stayed at a resort that promised something like "you won't even know you're in Cambodia." That's fine if that's what you want. But if you want to know you're in Vietnam, and be face-to-face with Vietnam most of your day, then stay in Danang, not Hoi An.

Third, for daily necessities, food, and anything else, Danang has a bigger and cheaper selection. For Vietnamese people, staying in Hoi An would feel like staying inside Disneyland—and being limited to the inside-amusement-park selection of goods and paying inside-amusement-park prices for everything. Anywhere near the Old Town, it's not easy to buy any kind of daily necessities, because every shop space is massage or tours or a tourist trap of some kind.

Fourth, beaches. Hoi An has only a marginally acceptable beach, Cua Dai (Big Crab):

https://maps.app.goo.gl/2DrpN4dTS67p6uG9A

Danang has bigger and better beaches.

Fifth, Danang is a good starting point for all your adventures. Whether to Ba Na Hills or Marble Mountain or wherever else—Danang is a travel hub, and not just a tourist trap outpost.

Have I convinced you enough? If you still want to stay in Hoi An, I won't stop you. The main consideration for staying in Hoi An is to make sure your hotel is in (or at least walkably close to) the center of the Ancient City. Don't stay on the beach in Hoi An; the beach in Hoi An is much less nice than the beach in Danang, and it's too far to walk to the Ancient Town from the beach area. If you're going to stay in Hoi An, it should be for the Ancient Town.

Hotels in Hoi An Ancient Town? The main thing is location, because if you're in Ancient Town, you're probably going to be walking around and enjoying the ambience, not enjoying the hotel amenities. "Just one km outside the Ancient Town" is not a good location—it is probably on a dark road that's difficult to traverse at night. If you stay in Hoi An, make sure it's as close as possible to the Ancient Town. And you'll pay for that privilege. It's easy to spend as much as $300 per night or more in Hoi An. Back when Hoi An was an undiscovered place, hardcore backpackers loved getting those $5 per night hotel rooms; those days are long gone.

Whatever hotel you're interested in—and you have a huge selection on Tripadvisor, Expedia, Lonely Planet Forums, wherever—before you book it, go to Google Maps and verify that the location is close enough to the old town and not in the middle of a dark road. Don't trust what the fake reviews say. Also, as with most hotels in Vietnam, Agoda is the cheapest website for bookings. Often small Vietnamese hotels appear on Agoda and don't appear on Expedia. In other cases, Agoda's rates can be significantly cheaper than Expedia. As I mentioned previously in this book, Agoda is much better at dealing with Vietnamese hoteliers than Expedia is. The downside is that Agoda has terrible, or just nonexistent, customer service. Don't expect Agoda to have anyone you can contact for help, and don't expect them to step in if you have problems with your hotel. Also, the hotel reviews on their site are fake. Well, the reviews are real, but Agoda only publishes positive reviews, and deletes negative reviews.

If I've managed to convince you to stay in Danang and make a day trip to Hoi An, make sure your stay in Hoi An includes the sunset and evening hours. We Vietnamese people prefer to set out to Hoi An only in the afternoon, as there's not enough to do for a whole day, and the midday hours are generally too hot.

Walking through Hoi An Old Town

Walking is the only way to look around Hoi An Old Town; motorized vehicles are not allowed. Yes, it's a bit like Disneyland, but I already warned you about that—so enjoy it, because Disneyland can be fun too.

120K VND admission fee

Just like Disneyland, Hoi An Old Town now charges an admission fee, 120,000 VND per person just for going inside. (Depending on whom you ask, the fee may or may not apply to Vietnamese people.)

Although there is an official line that the 120,000 VND goes to historical preservation, I have doubts about that. Unless you mean repairs on some Party bigshot's mansion.

There are very variable, seemingly random booths and people coming up to foreigners at the bridges going into Old Town, asking for 120K VND for a ticket. It's so completely random, and usually only at one or two entrances. Most people, Vietnamese and foreign alike, just ignore those people. I suggest you either treat them like regular street scammers, or pretend you don't speak English or Vietnamese or Korean and have no idea what the heavens they're going on about. Or just go to a different entrance — although seriously, most people just ignore those ticket-askers and just walk right past them.

However, you will need one of those 120K VND tickets to see some of the old houses that are designated on the list. *Some? Which?* You might ask. The answer: highly variable, again. Various houses have guards posted at various times asking for a ticket. My guess is if you go early in the morning, there will be no guards and all the houses will be free. Note that your 120K VND does not give you admission to all the houses — only to five. It's on a tear-off-ticket system. That's probably so that people don't share or resell the tickets.

Here's a pretty good photo guide to the old houses you might want to see:

Wander

You don't really need to go inside those houses. There are lots of places to wander around in, and you can get a good enough view of very similar places that don't require an admission charge.

You should orient yourself with random wandering, stopping for a coffee or a beer when you feel like it. Keep your eyes on the Chinese inscriptions on the buildings: these were meeting and socializing halls for merchants' extended family associations. (Actually, the usual English translation is "clan," but I know that word has a bad connotation in American English.) The Chinese traders organized themselves around their extended family networks, which were themselves based on their Chinese sub-ethnicities and places of origin.

The biggest assembly hall corresponds to the Fujian people (also called Fukien, and I know the word sounds like something else in English), in Vietnamese called Phuc Kien. It's at 46 Tran Phu (you can also enter from Phan Chu Trinh). It contains a shrine to Thien Hau, the goddess who protects seafarers—you can see why she'd be important to Chinese traders in Hoi An—and she is the same seafarers' goddess to whom shrines are built in Saigon. She is accompanied by shrines to Thien Ly Nhan (goddess of distant vision) and Thuong Phong Nhi (god of distant hearing)—again, you can guess how interested seafarers would be in having distant vision and distant hearing. Like most of the organized sights in Hoi An, the Phuc Kien assembly hall closes around 5 P.M.—so if you come only for the evening lights, you'll miss out on the organized attractions.

Another "must see" sight is the Tan Ky old house. Yes, a family actually lives upstairs; they claim to be the seventh generation descended from the trader Tan Ky. That also means that you can't go upstairs (so nosy!), but it's still an interesting look around, at least if you haven't been in a million old Vietnamese houses before. It's two hundred years old, which for many parts of the world, isn't that old. Still interesting. Don't forget to look at the carved ceiling, and at the flood water-level markings on the walls. My favorite part of this house, as of all old well-off Vietnamese houses, is the central courtyard, with bedrooms that have balconies onto the courtyard. The light and ventilation that courtyard provides are amazing. The house is at 101 Nguyen Thai Hoc.

As you're walking around, you will likely be offered *banh xoai*. They're mango-shaped rice balls, like mochi, with crushed peanuts inside. The local price is 3 rice balls for 20K. They are delicious. Try them.

You'll also likely be offered a boat ride. It's not a bad idea, although I think it's too hot to attempt in the middle of the day—much more comfortable in the evening or late afternoon, or do it Vietnamese style and go at 7 A.M.!

There are boat ride ticket vendors all around selling a 20 or 30 minute ride for 170K VND, and when you hesitate, they'll reduce it to 150K VND. A good wage for a guy like a boat rower is 20K VND per hour (or twice that if he can speak English). Moreover, my guess is the boat rower doesn't get much or even anything from that 150K-170K, and he will ask you for tips. I suggest you just try approaching some of the boat guys directly and offer them something like 100K for a one-hour ride.

Be very clear on the price, because some boat drivers magically pretend to have had a misunderstanding and claim that e.g. you agreed to pay 1,000,000 when you actually only agreed to 100,000.

The other thing you might be offered? Floating candle lanterns to float on the water in the evening! Be very careful with your fingers when maneuvering to set it down in the water — those are well known for causing minor hand burns. And thanks to the dominance of the tourist economy, there isn't even a medical clinic anywhere around Old Town.

Eat and drink

Hoi An is famous for banh mi. It's the same crispy, stick-like banh mi I showed you in Danang, called banh mi que. There's a banh mi shop called Phuong that showed up on Anthony Bourdain's TV show.

https://maps.app.goo.gl/1c2kZaR8jwmVz23T9

While Bourdain never claims that the places he shows are the best, only that they're a sample of what's available, tourists don't read the fine print, and flock and flock—so now Phuong is overrun by tourists and gets by on her Bourdain reputation, rather than on the quality of the banh mi. Skip Phuong, I say, and go for her competitor Madam Khanh at 115 Tran Cao Van.

https://maps.app.goo.gl/QKxAXynAGhpsHx1JA

It's been Vietnamese people's favorite in Hoi An since long before Bourdain. It's not as touristy as Phuong, but still touristy enough so that they should be able to understand your order in English. (If you want vegetarian, the magic Vietnamese word is *chay*.)

Back in the day, both Phuong and Khanh were just street carts. Now they're both full-on restaurants.

After sunset, watch the lanterns, have a coffee or beer, watch the candle lanterns float down the river, and, of course, have dinner. Yes, there are a million places competing for your business. Yes, all the resorts have fancy restaurants. Yes, there are touts promising you the best meal of your life. But I'm going to tell you where Vietnamese people love to eat and drink in Hoi An Old Town: Mot Hoi An (*mot* means *one*) at 150 Tran Phu

https://maps.app.goo.gl/JntEsVDTZhc53utRA

They started their fame with their *nuoc thao* which is a Chinese/ Vietnamese herbal drink whose name literally translates to *grass juice*. But now their food is equally famous: cao lau (Hoi An noodles like mi quang), chicken rice (boiled chicken with rice, a dish popularized by Fujianese traders in Hoi An), pho (that one's for the tourists), and a huge banh mi sandwich. That and their amazing drinks. They don't advertise. They don't hassle you on the street. They're popular with all Vietnamese twentysomethings. Please go there.

They do get crowded. Another good place for food — more street, and not as delicious as Mot, but still pretty good, and not at all touristy — is a corner street stall called Man.

https://maps.app.goo.gl/SFQWMxygh1Rh8D2x5

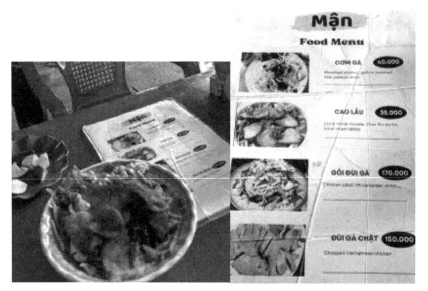

I also have a super mega ultra local coffee shop to recommend to you. It never sees tourists. It's just the side of a house, the inside of which is a tailor shop, serving local customers.

Cafe Lia

https://maps.app.goo.gl/kaMGieozgEViCDz19

They play old (before we were gloriously liberated) South Vietnamese music, they do have egg coffee and all kinds of tourist and local favorites, and the owner is a cool guy who speaks English well. When you're looking for Lia, don't look at the house frontage on the main street. Look at the frontage that's inside the alley. Though Lia does have a sign on the main street.

And as you get a bit away from the tourist center of Old Town, you'll find more interesting places. Like this super-comfy, super-atmospheric cafe, called Ren Rua. The name means *What's up?* in the local Danang dialect.

https://maps.app.goo.gl/sVLwfwBLZse6acEm6

Hoi An Tailors

Yes, there are tailor shops in Hoi An. It's a cliche by now. Twenty years ago, tailors in Hoi An were a bargain only known by the most intrepid world travelers. Nowadays, almost all Hoi An tailors are tourist traps that focus on making the sale, then outsourcing the actual sewing of your clothes to the lowest bidder. The people you see in the shop are not the people sewing your clothes.

If you want to get clothes made in Vietnam, generally Saigon or Hanoi would be a better choice than Hoi An. Saigon and Hanoi tailors are focused on repeat business, not on passing tourists. We Vietnamese people certainly have our clothes made in Saigon or Hanoi, at least if that's where we live. Tailors in Hoi An have developed a well-reserved reputation over the past few years for catering to tourists—focusing on marketing and on clothes that look good enough for the tourist picking them up, and then who cares what happens once the tourist leaves town.

But there's one Hoi An tailor shop that comes highly recommended from local Hoi An people I know. Several people told me that this is the one they trust. And Tripadvisor seems to concur, as do the Vietnamese-language review websites. You may also want to ask your *guy*, though I haven't discussed tailors with either *guy* I recommend here. The average Grab driver, who was probably a farmer or factory worker being driving a Grab car, likely wouldn't know much about tailoring, but the two *guys* I recommend both used to have white-collar engineering jobs, so I think they might know something about tailoring.

Their advice might be the same as mine. Go to Saigon or Danang for good tailoring. But if you want to get clothes in Hoi An, then go for it. Just note that because 99% of their traffic is from tourists, the clothes they make for you will not last. But they're cheap enough that maybe you shouldn't care. Some relatives of mine got some ridiculous fruit-print-design suits at Thanh Van, to wear just for fun, just for their trip to Vietnam — they paid something like $150 per suit, and for that money, they got their money's worth and were able to wear the suits for a few weeks, then throw them away. Expect that from any Hoi An tailor.

Anyway, the shop that I've heard good things about is Thanh Van at 75 Tran Hung Dao.

https://maps.app.goo.gl/jj1sLqser2j86B428

It's literally next door to Kimmy. Kimmy is one of the less-bad tailors in Hoi An, but it's still a tourist trap. Thanh Van is better and cheaper. Yes, they can make suits, or ao dai (those long Vietnamese dresses—for men as well as women!), dresses, shirts, or anything else you need. They can also copy clothes you bring in, whether you bring the actual item you want copied or a photo of it, perhaps from a magazine. Now, note that Thanh Van is still a Hoi An tailor. You won't get excellent quality. But you'll get something cheap and cheerful. That's all you can hope for.

I think many visitors to Vietnam have never had tailored clothes made back in their countries, and don't realize that it takes some time and some fittings. Yes, it's possible to make a suit or a dress in one hour, but it won't fit very well—and fitting very well is supposedly the point of tailoring. An honest tailor, like the one I recommend here, will tell you how many days and fittings are needed; if you won't be in town long enough, take the hint and don't try to rush the tailoring process, because the result will be worse than ready-to-wear clothes from Walmart.

Hoi An Tailors, including the less-bad ones like Thanh Van are far worse in quality and higher in price than Saigon and Hanoi tailors. If for some reason you don't like Thanh Van, then don't go to other tailors in Hoi An, who pretty much universally have high prices and low quality; just go to a tailor in Saigon or Hanoi, or wait until you're back in your home country.

And, of course, Hoi An tailors, including Thanh Van, are notorious for paying commissions and hiring shills, so don't believe anyone who has a great tailor to recommend. How can you trust that I'm not getting a commission from Thanh Van? Because I'm not asking you to tell them that Elly sent you. In fact, they have no idea who I am, so don't even try to tell them that Elly sent you.

Love it

Enjoy Danang and Hoi An the way a local would—the way this book has, I hope, taught you to enjoy them. If with my Vietnamese-person-centric recommendations I've sometimes brought you slightly out of your usual travel comfort zone, maybe that's a good thing? I hope I've broadened your perspective beyond what you can find on regular travel websites and in regular guidebooks.

Final bit of advice and warning: There's a branch of Pho 24, which serves literally Vietnam's worst pho, at the Danang airport. Please don't eat there. I'd hate for that to ruin your Danang experience.

You might be expecting a pitch for my other guidebooks—guidebook authors always do that at the end—but here's a pitch that's more about my hometown than about my book: if you liked Danang, you'll love Saigon! It's bigger and faster-moving than Danang, and I love it. In my heart of hearts, I believe you haven't really been to Vietnam if you haven't been to Saigon, but I'll keep that opinion to myself—ah, oops, I just wrote it here.

Enjoy Vietnam. Enjoy Danang. Even enjoy the tourism overload that is Hoi An. If something disappoints you, remember that no place is perfect, and that most Vietnamese people grew up in rural poverty—so be patient and try to be understanding.

Have fun, and remember to bring a warm jacket in the winter.

Also by Elly Thuy Nguyen

My Saigon
My Saigon: The Local Guide to Ho Chi Minh City, Vietnam
Secrets to Live in Vietnam on $500 a Month
Da Nang and Hoi An, Vietnam
Dating Vietnamese Women
Happy in Hanoi: The Local Guide to Hanoi, Vietnam
Undiscovered Quy Nhon: The Local Guide to Vietnam's Beach Paradise
Discover Dalat: Local Travel Guide to Da Lat, Vietnam

About the Author

Elly Thuy Nguyen is a devoted Saigon nerd. Saigon is her major hobby. Reading and writing are her other hobbies, and also her vocation: in her day job, Elly is an English-language marketing writer. In addition to her love of Saigon and the written word, Elly enjoys cafes, cats, hip-hop, and international travel.

Made in the USA
Coppell, TX
08 February 2025

45570977R00095